SPECTRUM

WORKBOOK 6

A Communicative Course in English

David P. Rein
with Donald R. H. Byrd

Donald R. H. Byrd *Project Director*

Prentice Hall Regents
Englewood Cliffs, NJ 0,__

D1401965

Project Manager: Nancy L. Leonhardt
Manager of Development Services: Louisa B. Hellegers
Development Editor: Tünde A. Dewey
Contributing Writer: Samuela Eckstut

Director of Production and Manufacturing: David Riccardi
Editorial Production/Design Manager: Dominick Mosco
Electronic Production Coordinator: Molly Pike-Riccardi
Technical Support and Assistance: Rolando Corujo
Production Coordinator: Ray Keating

Cover Design: Roberto de Vicq
Interior Design: Anna Veltfort
Audio Editor: Andrew Gitzy

ACKNOWLEDGMENTS

Illustrations: pp. 4, 8, 10, 18, 21, 24, 44, 70, 72 by Anna Veltfort; pp. 20, 26, 28, and 66 by Constance Maltese; pp. 47, 48 by Kimble Pendleton; p. 23 by Sylvio Redinger; p. 42 by Randy Jones.

Photos: p. 6 Puppies at Humane Society pound by Michael Dwyer/Stock Boston, Inc., p.27 wooden bowl and spoons, briefcase, calculator, empty bookcase, and coat stand by Frank Labua; p. 46 Rock band performing by George Zimbel/Monkmeyer Press.

Printed in the United States of America
10 9 8 7 6

ISBN 0-13-830258-8

Prentice Hall International (UK) Limited, *London*
Prentice Hall of Australia Pty. Limited, *Sydney*
Prentice Hall Canada, Inc., *Toronto*
Prentice Hall Hispanoamericana, S.A., *Mexico*
Prentice Hall of India Private Limited, *New Delhi*
Prentice Hall of Japan, Inc., *Tokyo*
Simon & Schuster Asia Pte. Ltd, *Singapore*
Editora Prentice Hall do Brasil, Ltda., *Rio de Janeiro*

INTRODUCTION

Spectrum 6 represent the sixth level of a six-level course designed for adolescent and adult learners of English. The student books, workbooks, and audio cassette programs for each level provide practice in all four communication skills, with a special focus on listening and speaking. The first four levels are offered in split editions—1A, 1B, 2A, 2B, 3A, 3B, 4A, and 4B. The student books, workbooks, teacher's editions, and audio programs for levels 1 to 4 are also available in full editions.

Spectrum is a "communicative" course in English, based on the idea that communication is not merely an end-product of language study, but rather the very process through which a new language is acquired. Since the starting point for communication is understanding, the student books, workbooks, and audio program emphasize the importance of comprehension, both as a useful skill and as a natural means of acquiring a language. *Spectrum* considers interaction to be another vital step in language acquisition. Student books offer both focused and open-ended interactive practice. Workbooks offer written practice of new functions and structures and guided composition activities preparing students for written interaction.

Workbook 6 is closely coordinated with **Student Book 6**. Both consist of twelve units divided into one- , two- and three-page lessons. Review lessons follow Units 1 to 6 and Units 7 to 12. The workbook provides listening and writing practice to reinforce material introduced in the corresponding student book lesson:

- The first two or three exercises in each unit are based on the reading in the textbook. The activities are designed to develop students' reading skills as well as their vocabulary and call for written responses.

- The one-page comprehension lesson in the student book leads to a variety of listening activities in the workbook designed to focus students' attention on functions, structures, and aspects of pronunciation. All listening activities are recorded on cassette.

- For each thematic lesson in the student book, students complete workbook exercises offering additional writing practice on new functions and structures.

- In the last exercise of each unit students write paragraphs or letters based on authentic models. The activities are related thematically or fundtionally to the corresponding textbook unit. In many of these exercises students can use personal information.

Audio Cassette Program 6 offers two cassettes for the student book and one cassette for the workbook. All listening activities are dramatized by professional actors in realistic recordings with sound effects.

In addition to step-by-step instructions for the student book, **Teacher's Edition 6** contains listening scripts and answer keys for the workbook.

REVIEWERS AND CONSULTANTS

Regents/Prentice Hall would like to thank the following long-time users of *Spectrum*, whose insights and suggestions have helped to shape the content and format of the new edition: Motofumi Aramaki, *Sony Language Laboratory*, Tokyo, Japan; *Associacão Cultural Brasil-Estados Unidos* (*ACBEU*), Salvador-Bahia, Brazil; *AUA Language Center*, Bangkok, Thailand, Thomas J. Kral and faculty; Pedro I. Cohen, Professor Emeritus of English, Linguistics, and Education, *Universidad de Panamá*; *ELSI Taiwan Language Schools*, Taipei, Taiwan, Kenneth Hou and faculty; James Hale, *Sundai ELS*, Tokyo, Japan; *Impact*, Santiago, Chile; *Instituto Brasil-Estados Unidos* (*IBEU*), Rio de Janeiro, Brazil; *Instituto Brasil-Estados Unidos No Ceará* (*IBEU-CE*), Fortaleza, Brazil; *Instituto Chileno Norteamericano de Cultura*, Santiago, Chile; *Instituto Cultural Argentino Norteamericano* (*ICANA*), Buenos Aires, Argentina; Christopher M. Knott, *Chris English Masters Schools*, Kyoto, Japan; *The Language Training and Testing Center*, Taipei, Taiwan, Anthony Y. T. Wu and faculty; *Lutheran Language Institute*, Tokyo, Japan; *Network Cultura, Ensino e Livraria Ltda*, São Paulo, Brazil; *Seven Language and Culture*, São Paulo, Brazil.

CONTENTS

UNIT		PAGES	UNIT		PAGES
1	Lesson 1	1	**5**	Lesson 21	25
	Lesson 2	2		Lesson 22	26
	Lessons 3–4	3–5		Lessons 23–24	27–29
	Lesson 5	6		Lesson 25	30
2	Lesson 6	7	**6**	Lesson 26	31
	Lesson 7	8		Lesson 27	32
	Lessons 8–9	9–11		Lessons 28–29	33–35
	Lesson 10	12		Lesson 30	36
3	Lesson 11	13		Review of units 1–6	37–40
	Lesson 12	14			
	Lessons 13–14	15–17			
	Lesson 15	18			
4	Lesson 16	19			
	Lesson 17	20			
	Lessons 18–19	21–23			
	Lesson 20	24			

CONTENTS

UNIT		PAGES
7	Lesson 31	41
	Lesson 32	42
	Lessons 33–34	43–45
	Lesson 35	46
8	Lesson 36	47
	Lesson 37	48
	Lessons 38–39	49–51
	Lesson 40	52
9	Lesson 41	53
	Lesson 42	54
	Lessons 43–44	55–57
	Lesson 45	58
10	Lesson 46	59
	Lesson 47	60
	Lessons 48–49	61–63
	Lesson 50	64

UNIT		PAGES
11	Lesson 51	65
	Lesson 52	66
	Lessons 53–54	67–69
	Lesson 55	70
12	Lesson 56	71
	Lesson 57	72
	Lessons 58–59	73–75
	Lesson 60	76
	Review of units 7–12	77–80

UNIT 1 · LESSONS 1–5

Lesson 1

1 ▶ **Refer to the reading on page 2 of your textbook. Decide whether each statement is *for* or *against* construction of space stations.**

_____*for*_____ 1. Space stations can be used more than once to make space travel much less expensive.

_____ 2. However, more experimentation is needed.

_____ 3. However, money could be better spent to improve people's quality of life right here on Earth.

_____ 4. But the costs will be far less than the benefits.

_____ 5. Moreover, spacecraft could be launched much more cheaply than from Earth.

_____ 6. Besides, space stations open the possibility of space cities.

_____ 7. But there has been a lot of criticism and budget cutbacks.

_____ 8. Even so, many scientists look forward to using Freedom as a spaceport for peopled trips to Mars.

2 ▶ **The words in the box can be used as either nouns or verbs with no change in spelling or form. Complete the sentences, using the words from the box.**

experience	regard	circle	figure	panic	split
sense	supply	price	tape	share	base

1. I _____*figure*_____ that whatever will be will be.

2. Each winner's _____ of the lottery prize was $10,000.

3. _____ is the best teacher.

4. The world's _____ of natural fuels, such as coal, wood, and oil, is diminishing rapidly.

5. Because of bad weather, our plane had to _____ the airport for twenty minutes before landing.

6. _____ is your worst enemy in an emergency.

7. I'm going to _____ your final grade on your attendance, your test grades, and your participation in class.

8. If you think positively, it's possible to _____ a defeat as a victory.

9. After we've rehearsed a few more times, we'll be ready to make a _____ of our performance.

10. Many animals can _____ danger more quickly than people.

Lesson 2

1 ► **Two business executives are talking about whether their company should hire any new employees. Listen to their discussion and answer the questions. Choose *a* or *b*. Then complete each sentence.**

1. _____*Some*_____ new employees were added to the staff last month.

   a. No   (b.) Some

2. _____ employees have left the company or retired since then.

   a. No   b. Some

3. _____ wants to hire another employee.

   a. The man   b. The woman

4. _____ being transferred to the plant in Kingston.

   a. One person is   b. Several people are

5. The woman wishes she had _____ .

   a. known about the transfer   b. been transferred, too

2 ► **A father and his teenaged son disagree about the son's loud music. Listen to their discussion. Then, in your own words, summarize the major points each one makes.**

The father said that *the music was too loud,* _____

_____

_____

   The son said that _____

_____

_____

_____

3 ► **A man wants to use a credit card to buy a stereo. His wife wants them to save and pay cash. Listen to their discussion. Then, in your own words, summarize the major points each one makes.**

The wife said that *the stereo costs almost $800, and* _____

_____

_____

_____

   The husband said that _____

_____

_____

_____

_____

Lessons 3-4

1 ► **Match each conjunction with its use in a discussion or a debate.**

_a_   1. besides   a. to support an argument

_____   2. but   b. to counter an argument

_____   3. even so   c. to draw a conclusion

_____   4. furthermore

_____   5. however

_____   6. moreover

_____   7. nevertheless

_____   8. so

_____   9. therefore

_____   10. what's more

2 ► **Classify the conjunctions in exercise 1 as less formal and more formal.**

1. less formal: _____*besides*_____ , _____ ,

_____ , _____ , _____ ,

2. more formal: _____ , _____ ,

_____ , _____ , _____

3 ► **These are arguments people used in a discussion about whether workers should have to retire at a certain age. First complete the sentences with less formal conjunctions. Then rewrite the arguments as they might appear in formal writing, using semicolons.**

1. Older workers are still able to do a full day's work. _____*Besides*_____ , they have a lot of valuable experience to offer.

_____

_____

2. They don't necessarily have to be paid more than younger workers because they have worked longer. _____ , they're often more dedicated to the company.

_____

_____

3. They may have some health problems, _____ young people can also have health problems.

_____

_____

4. Some workers are not that vigorous in their seventies and eighties. _____ , many still are.

_____

_____

4 ▶ **Read the magazine article. What benefits do you think a company should offer workers with young children? Write a paragraph using ideas from the reading and your own opinions. Use at least three of these conjunctions:** *furthermore, moreover, however, nevertheless,* **and** *therefore.*

GREAT COMPANIES
TO WORK FOR

Few companies offer such benefits as child-care centers on site, flexible schedules, and work-at-home arrangements; however, there are exceptions. A few employers lead the rest in making it easier to have a job and raise a family at the same time. You can use our description of the benefits they offer to evaluate those of your own company or a company you are considering working for.

• **Amcom, Inc.** Employees of this computer manufacturer must be at work from 10 A.M. to 2 P.M. Except for those hours, however, they may choose their own working times to suit themselves. For computer programmers and software writers who want to work full time at home, the company provides terminals and gives full pay.

• **Carswell, Inc.** Employees at the headquarters of this food-processing company can put their children under five years of age in the company's on-site day-care center, for a cost of $60 a week. Working women get two months off, at full pay, to have children; moreover, working parents get six months of unpaid child-care leave.

• **General Products.** This 74-year-old clothing manufacturer offers its employees a program ...

I think a company should _____

_____

_____

_____

_____

_____

_____

5 ▶ **Read about these people. Then complete the sentences appropriately.**

1. Michelle Renard is sorry she took chemistry. She's failed several tests this semester, but she may have passed the last one.

   Michelle hopes *she passed the last chemistry test* _____ .

   She wishes _____

   _____ .

2. Emmanual Amadife just had a job interview. He regrets that he didn't wear a suit. He's worried that he dressed inappropriately.

   Emmanual hopes _____

   _____ .

   He wishes _____

   _____ .

3. Elliot Winters was waiting for a phone call from his brother, but he had to go out on an errand. When he returned, he heard the phone stop ringing as he walked in the front door.

   Elliot hopes _____

   _____ .

   He wishes _____

   _____ .

6 ▶ **Express regrets about some things you've done and haven't done in your life so far. Complete each statement below. Then add another that explains or elaborates on the first.**

1. I wish I'd *majored in medicine. I'd like to work in a hospital, but I don't have the* _____

   background for it. _____

   _____

2. I wish I'd _____

   _____

   _____

3. I wish I'd _____

   _____

   _____

4. I wish I hadn't _____

   _____

   _____

5. I wish I hadn't _____

   _____

   _____

Lesson 5

▶ **Write a rebuttal to the editorial. You might want to use some of the arguments in the box.**

— cruel and inhumane/animals cannot tell you their pain
— excessive pain/broken limbs and mutilations
— unnecessary experimentation with products such as make-up
— computers can be used as an alternative
— humans have superior intelligence/should protect those with less intelligence, not exploit and kill them

I think it is O.K. to use animals in laboratory experiments. Using animals allows scientists to find out about disease and injuries in order to help humans. Besides, the anatomy of some animals is very similar to that of human beings, which means that animals can be used instead of humans. Furthermore, most of the animals that are used in laboratories are homeless, and using them for needed scientific experiments helps to decrease the number of stray animals on the streets. Many of the medicines and treatments in the past few years have been developed through careful animal testing. I hope that we have learned by now that science needs these animal experiments. Just where are our priorities anyway—with humans or animals?

_____

_____

_____

_____

_____

_____

_____

_____

_____

_____

_____

— _____

_____

Lesson 6

1 ▸ **Refer to the reading on pages 12–13 of your textbook. Mark an _X_ next to the statements that could probably be made by people who knew Jesse Owens well.**

_X_ 1. He was a man with a great deal of physical courage. He performed even when he was in pain.

_____ 2. He couldn't imagine being discriminated against.

_____ 3. Wherever he went, he was recognized and appreciated, so he considered himself important.

_____ 4. Whatever happened to him, he kept going. He wasn't a man who gave up easily.

_____ 5. He found it difficult to accept that Hitler didn't congratulate him for his Olympic victories. He would have enjoyed the recognition.

_____ 6. Whenever he had the opportunity to race, he took it, although he was bothered by the nature of some of his competition.

_____ 7. He was patriotic to his country in spite of the treatment he received from some people there.

2 ▸ **Complete the paragraph below with adjectives from the list in the box. Some items have more than one possible answer.**

accidental	historic
basic	national
critical	natural
cultural	nonprofessional
heroic	Olympic

The _____ _Olympic_ _____ Games are held every four years with the

_____ purpose of bringing together athletes from all over the

world. These men and women must be _____ athletes. Although

many people have been _____ of some aspects of the Olympics,

the Games have kept their _____ value: an opportunity for athletes

of different _____ and _____

backgrounds to understand each other better through healthy competition.

Lesson 7

1 ▶ Mrs. Reilly is interviewing David Mitchell and Mark Robinson for a job as a drugstore clerk. Listen to the interviews. Choose *a* or *b*. Then complete each sentence.

First interview

1. One reason David wants the job is that he *has to help out at home* .

   a. wants to save money for college   (b.) has to help out at home

2. David enjoys _____.

   a. working with people   b. telling other people what to do

3. David seems to be _____.

   a. unfriendly and reserved   b. friendly and outgoing

4. David considers himself _____.

   a. reliable   b. irresponsible

5. David thinks Mrs. Reilly would find him _____.

   a. honest and hardworking   b. untrustworthy and unambitious

Second interview

6. One reason Mark wants the job is that he _____.

   a. likes to talk to people   b. enjoys responsibility

7. Mark considers himself _____.

   a. cooperative and patient   b. easygoing and creative

8. Mark _____ imagine himself making things.

   a. can   b. can't

2 ▶ If you were Mrs. Reilly, would you hire David or Mark? Complete the paragraphs.

If I were Mrs. Reilly, I'd hire _____ because _____

_____

_____

_____

_____

I wouldn't hire _____ because _____

_____

_____

_____

_____

_____

Lessons 8–9

1 ▶ **Complete the conversations below with words from the box.**

ambitious	friendly	insecure	modest	self-confident
conceited	hardworking	irresponsible	outgoing	unimaginative
creative	honest	lazy	reliable	

1. **A** Maria seems very ambitious, doesn't she?
   B Yes, she's certainly ___hardworking___ .
   A She's so industrious that everybody else
   in the department seems _____
   _____
   by contrast.

2. **A** Robert considers himself creative.
   B Is he serious? He's one of the most
   _____
   people I've ever worked with. I don't
   think he's had an original idea in years.

3. **A** How would you describe yourself?
   B If it didn't sound _____
   to say so, I'd describe myself as modest!

4. **A** I enjoy working alone. I can't imagine
   myself working with other people. I'm
   just not _____
   enough.
   B That's strange. You've always seemed
   friendly to me.

5. **A** People are funny. Ray considers himself
   _____ ,
   but he's one of the most reliable workers
   we have.
   B And everyone finds Barbara very
   self-confident, yet she tells me that
   underneath she's extremely_____
   _____ .

   A If only we could see ourselves the way
   others see us!

2 ▶ **Two coworkers are talking about who will be named head of their department. Complete their conversation by matching one item from Column A with one item from Column B.**

Column A	Column B
Have you ever watched her	act like that
heard her	deal with clients
I can't imagine her	department head
I find her	feel uncomfortable
I've never seen her	running the department
she makes me	talk about them afterward
Who do you think they're going to appoint	very hardworking and responsible

A _Who do you think they're going to appoint department head_ _____ ?

B I don't know, but I hope it isn't Lisa. _____
_____

A Why not?_____
_____

B Maybe so, but somehow _____
_____ . She's insincere. _____
_____ and then _____ ?

She's like two different people.

A No, _____ . I still thinks she'd do a great job.

3 ▶ **In the chart below, check (✔) the form(s) that can follow each verb.**

SOME VERBS AND THEIR POSSIBLE COMPLEMENTS

VERB	NOUN	ADJECTIVE	BASE FORM OF VERB	PROGRESSIVE FORM OF VERB
appoint	✔			
call				
consider				
elect				
find				
hear				
imagine				
keep				
make				
see				
watch				

4 ▶ **Complete the conversation, using question words with *-ever*.**

A What do you want to do this weekend?

B I don't care. _____*Whatever*_____ you want to do.

A I'd like to invite some people over for a barbecue. Who do you think we should ask?

B _____ you want. Anybody's O.K. with me.

A Should we have hamburgers, hot dogs, or both?

B I don't know. Hamburgers. Or hot dogs. _____ one you want is all right.

A Do you think we should have the barbecue Saturday or Sunday?

B _____ you say. I don't have any plans for either day.

A Should we set up the barbecue in the usual place, or under the tree for a change?

B I'll put it _____ you want it. It doesn't make any difference to me.

A You know what I like about you? You're so decisive. You'll agree with _____ I say.

5 ▶ **Read the weekly horoscope and the conversations. Then decide which sign of the zodiac each speaker was born under.**

1. **A** Have you read your horoscope for this week?
   B Yes, but I don't think it's very accurate. I can't think of anything I've learned in the last few months. How about yours?
   A I agree that it isn't very accurate. I mean, have you ever seen me overreact? What are they talking about? How could they say something like that? I'm always calm!

   A *Capricorn*

   B _____

2. **A** What did you think of your horoscope?
   B Maybe I am typical of my sign. I can't imagine letting someone else be the leader. I always like to be in charge. Are you typical, too?
   A I don't think so. I consider myself pretty easygoing. I don't think I have any enemies, and even if I did, I wouldn't be interested in getting back at them for whatever they'd done.

   A _____

   B _____

3. **A** I'm sorry I read my horoscope this morning.
   B Why?
   A You know the problem I've been having with one of my coworkers? It's supposed to get even worse!
   B Uh-oh. Speaking of work, I wish they'd call me from Fonex. I want to know whether I got the job.
   A So that's why you've been so hard to get along with lately. Hey, come to think of it, I think your horoscope said something about that. Let me check…. This is amazing! How did they know about you and Fonex?

   A _____

   B _____

WEEKLY HOROSCOPE

CAPRICORN (December 22–January 20): Although you tend to overreact to situations, this is a time to stay unusually calm, especially regarding financial commitments.

AQUARIUS (January 21–February 18): Waiting for the result of a job interview is making you nervous and difficult to live with. But a new position at this time would not be advantageous to you, so try not to be impatient and uncooperative with your present coworkers.

PISCES (February 19–March 20): This week you will be extremely imaginative and creative. You are ready to put to use whatever you have learned and experienced in recent months.

ARIES (March 21–April 20): You consider yourself a good judge of character, but you made a mistake recently that could cost you both emotionally and financially. Be more careful this week.

TAURUS (April 21–May 21): You will be faced with a decision that your usual indecisiveness will make difficult. However, no one can help you; only you can know how your decisions will affect your happiness and security.

GEMINI (May 22–June 21): You are involved in a business or personal relationship that should have ended long ago. Only your remarkable patience kept it going this long. This week you can expect to see the situation get even more difficult.

CANCER (June 22–July 23): You must try to accept situations as they are and not try to make them more comfortable for yourself. Others are being more honest with you than you know.

LEO (July 24–August 23): As a Leo, you are a natural leader: hardworking, ambitious, self-confident. But this week you will be indecisive and feel insecure, and you must let others take over the leadership role for a while.

VIRGO (August 24–September 23): You truly believe whatever you say, and you are exactly what you seem to be. You must be confident about your opinions, even when other people disagree.

LIBRA (September 24–October 23): You probably feel that someone who owes you a great deal doesn't appreciate all that you've done. Be patient. Your work will be recognized.

SCORPIO (October 24–November 22): You are used to being independent, but this week will be a good time for you to work especially hard at cooperating with others. You won't be sorry.

SAGITTARIUS (November 23–December 21): If you are a typical Sagittarian, you want to pay back someone who has recently hurt you emotionally. Although you have some secret information about this person, now is not the time to use it. Your "enemy" will bring about his or her own downfall.

Lesson 10

► For which position do you consider yourself best suited? Write a short paragraph describing yourself and telling why you would be the right person for the job.

WANTED

INSURANCE SALESPERSON

Good verbal skills; must get along well with people and enjoy challenges. This is a real opportunity for the energetic person. The Acme Insurance Company

KINDERGARTEN ASSISTANT

Must like children and have a patient, helpful manner. Early morning hours needed. Kinderguard Center

HOSPITAL TECHNICIAN

A responsible person needed for independent laboratory work. Must have a good eye for details. This work requires someone who is careful. Institute Humana

SHOE STORE MANAGER

The right person will advance rapidly if he or she is ambitious, hardworking, and neat. Must be a good dresser with an eye for current fashion. Elite Footwear

NAME _____ COMPANY_____

_____

_____

_____

_____

_____

_____

_____

_____

_____

_____

Lesson 11

1 ▶ All of the underlined words below are from the reading on pages 22–23 of your textbook. Each of them can be used as more than one part of speech. Find each word in the appropriate paragraph of the reading. Then identify it as a noun, an adjective, or a verb.

1. In paragraph 1, <u>empty</u> is _an adjective_ .

2. In paragraph 1, <u>bargain</u> is _____ .

3. In paragraph 2, <u>exchange</u> is _____ .

4. In paragraph 3, <u>bargain</u> is _____ .

5. In paragraph 4, <u>cash</u> is _____ .

6. In paragraph 5, <u>play</u> is _____ .

7. In paragraph 6, <u>weekday</u> is _____ .

8. In paragraph 6, <u>plastic</u> is _____ .

9. In paragraph 7, <u>lives</u> is _____ .

10. In paragraph 8, <u>run</u> is _____ .

2 ▶ Complete the chart of related words.

adjective	noun
1. _available_	availability
2. complex	_____
3. _____	creativity
4. electric	_____
5. _____	flexibility
6. informal	_____
7. national	_____
8. responsible	_____
9. _____	specialty
10. uncertain	_____

Lesson 12

1 ▶ **Listen to the parts of seven conversations. In each, someone is trying to convince someone else. Match the conversation with the speakers.**

_a_ 1. first conversation   a. parent and child

_____ 2. second conversation   b. doctor and patient

_____ 3. third conversation   c. salesperson and customer

_____ 4. fourth conversation   d. teacher and student's parent

_____ 5. fifth conversation   e. husband and wife

_____ 6. sixth conversation   f. friends

_____ 7. seventh conversation   g. coworkers

2 ▶ **Listen again to the conversations in exercise 1. From the box, choose an appropriate ending for each and write it below.**

> Then I propose that we think it over for a few more days.
> Then it's important that you call me up and tell me what's happened.
> Of course. I suggest that you try it out and see what you think.
> It's essential that he do it, and I'd also like you to go over it with him.
> Nevertheless, I recommend that you be more careful in the future. Just a friendly warning.
> Thanks, but I really don't want to talk about it.
> In a case like that, it's crucial that she see me as soon as possible.

First conversation: _Then it's important that you call me up and tell me what's happened._

_____

Second conversation: _____

_____

Third conversation: _____

_____

Fourth conversation: _____

_____

Fifth conversation: _____

_____

Sixth conversation: _____

_____

Seventh conversation: _____

_____

Lessons 13–14

1 ► Mrs. Walker took her son Richard to the doctor today. Mr. Walker is asking her what the doctor said. Circle the correct form in parentheses.

A What did the doctor say about Richard?

B She says he (be, (is,) to be) better now, but it's important that he (get, gets, to get) plenty of rest.

A Is it necessary that he (take, takes, to take) any more medicine?

B No, but it's essential that he (drink, drinks, to drink) a lot of liquids. And she wants him (eat, eats, to eat) mostly soft food for the next couple of days.

A Did she recommend that he (go, goes, to go) back for another examination?

B She'd like one of us (take, takes, to take) him again Tuesday. She suggested that you (be, are, to be) the one this time; she'd like to meet you.

A Fine. I was going to propose that I (go, goes, to go), anyway.

2 ► First read the following information about first aid. Then imagine that three people are hiking when one is bitten by a snake. One person goes to look for trained medical help. The other stays to help the victim. What would you tell her to do if you were there? Use the information in the reading to complete the sentences.

If you are with someone who is bitten by a snake, follow these steps:

1. If possible, send someone for trained medical help at once. Look for one or more holes in the skin of the victim.

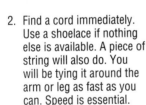

2. Find a cord immediately. Use a shoelace if nothing else is available. A piece of string will also do. You will be tying it around the arm or leg as fast as you can. Speed is essential.

3. Tie the cord above the wound, between the wound and the heart. Watch for swelling. As the swelling progresses, move the cord ahead of the swelling. Keep the cord loose enough to slip your finger under it.

4. You may make two cuts in the skin over the snake puncture marks to help remove the poison by suction. Avoid major nerves and blood vessels.

5. After incisions have been made, apply suction by mouth or with a small suction cup from a snakebite kit.

1. I'd recommend that she *look for one or more holes in the skin* .

2. I'd suggest that she _____
   _____ .

3. I'd insist that she _____
   _____ .

4. It's important that she _____
   _____ .

5. It's essential that she _____
   _____ .

6. It's crucial that she _____
   _____ .

3 ► **What do you think these people should do? Read about the situations and complete the sentences.**

1. Francis says he wants to lose weight, but he eats a lot of fattening foods and never exercises. If Francis really wants to lose weight, it's necessary that he *eat fewer fattening foods and get exercise* .

2. Milton says he wants a job, but when he goes for an interview, he's always late. He also wears inappropriate clothes and never asks any questions.

   If Milton really wants a job, it's essential that he

   _____

   _____

   _____ .

3. Gabriel has a room that he'd like to rent. However, he's asking too much money, and the room is dirty and needs painting.

   If Gabriel really wants to rent the room, I'd recommend that he _____

   _____

   _____ .

4 ► **Choose the correct forms in parentheses and write the sentences.**

1. If you're (worried about something, worried something about), it's often helpful to (talk about it, talk it about) with someone.

   If you're worried about something, _____

   _____

2. Take this form and (bring back it, bring it back) to me after you've (filled out it, filled it out).

   _____

   _____

3. The salesman told me that if I wasn't satisfied with the toaster, I could (take back it, take it back) to the store and (ask for a refund, ask a refund for).

   _____

   _____

4. I was especially glad to (run into Pam, run Pam into) this morning, because I hadn't (heard from her, heard her from) for a long time.

   _____

   _____

5 ▸ These conversations take place in an office. Complete them with two-word verbs from the box and pronouns. Be sure to use appropriate verb forms and place the pronouns correctly.

ask for	fill in/out	look for	plan for	talk about	turn off
bring back	get back	look up	put on	think about	turn on
call up	go over	pick out	run into	think over	worry about
figure out	hear from	pick up	take back	try out	write down

1. **A** I'm going to call Mr. King back now. Did you get his phone number?

   B I did, but I've forgotten it. I'm sorry. I knew I should have *written it down* .

2. **A** I can't get the copying machine to work again. I wish the salesman would come and _____ to the factory.

   B I think I see your problem. It would help if you _____ .
   It won't work if it's off.

3. **A** If those invoices are filled out, I'd like to _____
   with you before we send them out.

   B Pat was supposed to do them. I _____
   a few minutes ago, but she hadn't _____
   yet. As a matter of fact, she _____
   when I talked to her; she can't seem to find them.

6 ▸ The people who make these statements are trying to convince others of a course of action. Rewrite the underlined parts with such expressions as *I recommend that …* or *It's important that …* and two-word verbs. In some cases, more than one answer is possible.

1. If you're not happy with the dress, <u>you could return it</u> to the store.

   If you're not happy with the dress, I recommend (suggest) that you take it back
   to the store.

2. Since the form will be read by a machine, not a person, <u>you must complete it</u> accurately.

   _____

3. <u>I think you ought to consider it</u> for a few days if you're still unsure of your decision.

   _____

   _____

4. <u>We could review</u> the test results this afternoon at 2:30.

   _____

   _____

5. <u>You must be</u> careful and not <u>discuss</u> with anyone what happened.

   _____

   _____

Lesson 15

▶ **Write a short letter to Lee and try to convince him that he is making a big mistake.**

I suppose you have heard that I want to drop out of high school. Mother and Dad are against it, but I just don't have any interest in school anymore. The classes seem so boring to me, and the other students act like children. I know that it's important that I get an education, but I am working part-time in an auto parts store. I am already assistant to the manager, and I am making a good salary. My supervisor told me that I have a great future with the company. I have made up my mind to quit school, but I can't convince my parents. What do you recommend that I do?

Lee

Dear Lee,

_____

_____

_____

_____

_____

_____

_____

_____

_____

_____ ,

_____

Lesson 16

1 ▸ **Refer to the reading on page 32 of your textbook. Write *That's right*
or *That's wrong* for each statement below.**

_____*That's right.*_____ 1. The balloonists had crossed the Pacific before reaching

California.

_____ 2. Before putting down the drag ropes, they fired the separation

charge.

_____ 3. Ben Abruzzo was with two other passengers when the balloon

nearly crashed.

_____ 4. The balloonists started having problems several hours after

taking off from Nagashima, Japan.

_____ 5. While crossing the ocean, their balloon was covered with ice.

_____ 6. When the balloonists made their flight, it was the longest

balloon ride ever made.

_____ 7. After reaching 6,000 feet, the balloon suddenly started falling

at a rate of 1,500 feet a minute.

2 ▸ **Unscramble these words from the reading on page 32 of your textbook.
Then match each one with its meaning.**

1. lipers (title)   _____*perils*_____   a. do something that could be dangerous

2. kefofta (paragraph 2)   _____   b. sticking, adhering

3. ginilcgn (paragraph 3) _____   c. causes something to lose air

4. nlaidn (paragraph 4)   _____   d. very fast

5. kisr (paragraph 6)   _____   e. away from a body of water

6. tensced (paragraph 7)   _____   f. extreme dangers

7. dipar (paragraph 7)   _____   g. departure

8. sedfatel (paragraph 9) _____   h. drop, fall

Lesson 17

1 ▶ **A first-aid instructor is lecturing his class on the subject of choking. The pictures below illustrate what to do for a choking victim. Listen to the lecture. Then number the pictures in the order in which the instructor describes them.**

ⓐ _____

ⓑ _____

ⓒ _____

ⓓ _____

ⓔ _____1_____

ⓕ _____

2 ▶ **Listen again to the lecture on choking in exercise 1. Choose *a* or *b*. Then complete each sentence.**

1. Choking is an unusual medical emergency because it generally occurs when the victim is
   with other people .
   a. alone
   (b.) with other people

2. Choking _____ .
   a. happens mostly to old people   b. can happen to anyone

3. The musician Tommy Dorsey died of choking after _____ heavily.
   a. eating   b. drinking

4. U.S. President _____ was saved from choking on a peanut.
   a. Jimmy Carter   b. Ronald Reagan

5. A common cause of choking is _____ .
   a. false teeth   b. eating dry food such as bread

6. Learning the Heimlich maneuver takes _____ training.
   a. very little   b. a great deal of

7. When choking, you _____ use Heimlich's technique on yourself.
   a. can't   b. can

Lessons 18–19

1 ▸ **These are instructions for a game called "Concentration." Circle the correct choice in parentheses.**

This game requires two players and a standard deck of 52 cards. (First, Next), shuffle the cards thoroughly. (By then, Then), put the cards face down on a table, one at a time, in rows. Flip a coin to decide who goes first. (Next, By that time), the loser turns over any two cards, allowing the other player to see them. If the two cards are a pair — two kings, two fives, etc. — the first player keeps them and plays again. (Then, As soon as) that player fails to turn up a pair, both cards are replaced face down in their original position, and it's the other player's turn. (Finally, Once) all of the pairs have been removed, the game is over, and the player with the most cards has won.

2 ▸ **These are instructions for another game, "Earth, Air, Fire, and Water," which is played by a group. The instructions are not in the correct order. Rewrite them correctly as one paragraph, adding these time markers in the following order:** *First, Then, Next,* **and** *As soon as a player makes a wrong response.*

1. He or she trades places with the person in the center and a new round begins.
2. The person in the center throws a ball to anyone in the circle, calling out one of these words: "earth," "air," "fire," or "water."
3. The person who catches the ball has to give an appropriate response: for "earth," the name of an animal that walks; for "air," one that flies; for "water," one that swims; and no response for "fire." An animal may not be used more than once.
4. Form a circle and put one person in the center.

First, form a circle _____

_____

_____

_____

_____

_____

_____

3 ► Lana, a secretary, left these instructions for the person replacing her for part of a morning. Complete the instructions with appropriate time markers. Most items have more than one answer.

To my replacement —

Thank you for "filling in" for me while I'm at the dentist!

Unless Mrs. Eng has other instructions for you, please do the following:

_____First_____ , call Shore Realty at 8:30 A.M. sharp. Give them the message I've left attached.

_____ , type the letters on the right-hand side of the desk.

_____ , they're ready, take them to Mrs. Eng for her signature.

_____ , file the papers that are on the left-hand side of the desk.

_____ you've finished that, it will probably be time for a coffee break. The coffee wagon comes around 9:45, and the break lasts until 10:00.

Lana

4 ► Here are some rules for safe driving. Combine each pair of sentences with *Before ...*, *After ...*, or *When ...*, and an *-ing* form.

1. Start the engine. Check the rear-view mirror and the position of the driver's seat.

   Before starting the engine, check the rear-view mirror and the position of the driver's seat.

2. Drive. Check your mirror and speedometer frequently.

   _____

   _____

3. Drive in heavy traffic. Keep a safe distance.

   _____

   _____

4. Make a turn. Always signal.

   _____

   _____

5. Make a long trip. Drive for a couple of hours and then stop and rest.

   _____

   _____

5 ▶ **Rewrite the conversation, combining each pair of sentences in brackets [] into one sentence with *Before, After, When*, or *While*. Use *-ing* forms where possible.**

A How did you get interested in handwriting analysis?

B [I was waiting in the dentist's office one day. I read a magazine article about it.] [I read the article. I'd heard of graphology, but I didn't know very much about it.] [So then I thought about it for a while. I decided to take some courses.] [I finished those. I got a job right away analyzing the handwriting of job applicants at Mayco.]

A [And you were working there. You met Joe, right?]

B That's right. He was applying for a job there, and I fell in love with his handwriting!

A *How did you get interested in handwriting analysis?*

B *While waiting in the dentist's office one day, I read a magazine article about it.*

_____

_____

_____

_____

A _____

B _____

6 ▶ **Gilbert has decided to go on a diet. Complete the sentences with some good advice. Look at the pictures for ideas, and use the *-ing* form of each verb given.**

1. (go on diet)

   Before *going on a diet, you should see a doctor* _____ .

2. (diet)

   When _____ .

3. (try to lose weight)

   While _____ .

4. (lose weight)

   After_____ .

Lesson 20

▶ **You aren't home. Leave a note for a guest, telling him or her how to use a piece of electronic equipment or a household appliance.**

Steven,
    Here are the instructions on how to record a television program with my video cassette recorder. It's pretty easy to use. First, you turn on the TV. Then, you press the power on and insert the cassette. Then, you slide the switch to TUNER. After that, you press the TAPE/TV selector to TAPE. Select the channel you want to record. Next, you have to hold down the RECORD button while you press the PLAY button at the same time. Finally, press STOP when you have finished recording.

                    See you later,

                    Cliff

Directions

1. Turn TV on.
2. Press power to ON.
3. Insert cassette.
4. Set to TUNER.
5. Press TAPE/TV to TAPE.
6. Select channel to be recorded.
7. Hold RECORD, then press PLAY.
8. Press STOP when recording is completed.

_____ ,

_____

_____

_____

_____

_____

_____

_____

_____

_____

                            _____ ,

                            _____

Lesson 21

1 ► **In each pair of sentences, *a* is from the reading on pages 42–43 of your textbook. Does *b* have the same meaning or a different meaning? Write *Same* or *Different*.**

Different

1. a. The Romans, in turn, applied Greek theory on an even grander scale to build magnificent highways and viaducts, public baths, and elaborate sewage systems. (paragraph 2)
   b. The Greeks added to what they had learned from the Romans and built even more impressive highways, viaducts, public baths, and sewage systems.

2. a. Less well known are the road-building activities of South America's Incas, who flourished during the fifteenth century. (paragraph 3)
   b. The road-building activities of South America's Incas, who flourished during the fifteenth century, are less well known.

3. a. The Incas were also great bridge builders. (paragraph 4)
   b. The Incas were builders of large bridges, as well as roads.

4. a. Regularly during the Middle Ages and Renaissance, Europe became excited over "inventions" that had originated in China centuries earlier and had migrated slowly westward to Europe. (paragraph 7)
   b. During the Middle Ages and Renaissance, Europeans often thought they were seeing something new, when actually it had come from the Chinese, who had had it hundreds of years before.

2 ► **Rewrite the paragraph below. Where possible, combine nouns or adverbs with past participles to form noun modifiers.**

I am fortunate to live in this house that I love so much. Unusual in this part of the world, it is a house that has eight sides. It was built over a century ago by my great-grandfather, from bricks that were made by hand. Looking out of my front windows that are shaded by trees, I can see gardens that are kept well, fields of wheat that are warmed by the sun and that were just cut, and hills that are covered with green.

I am fortunate to live in this much-loved house.

Lesson 22

1 ► Jim and Carol are moving into a new apartment and trying to decide how to arrange their furniture. They're looking at drawings of the rooms and measurements of their furniture. Listen to their conversation. Fill in the blanks with dimensions. Then draw the furniture where they finally decide to put it.

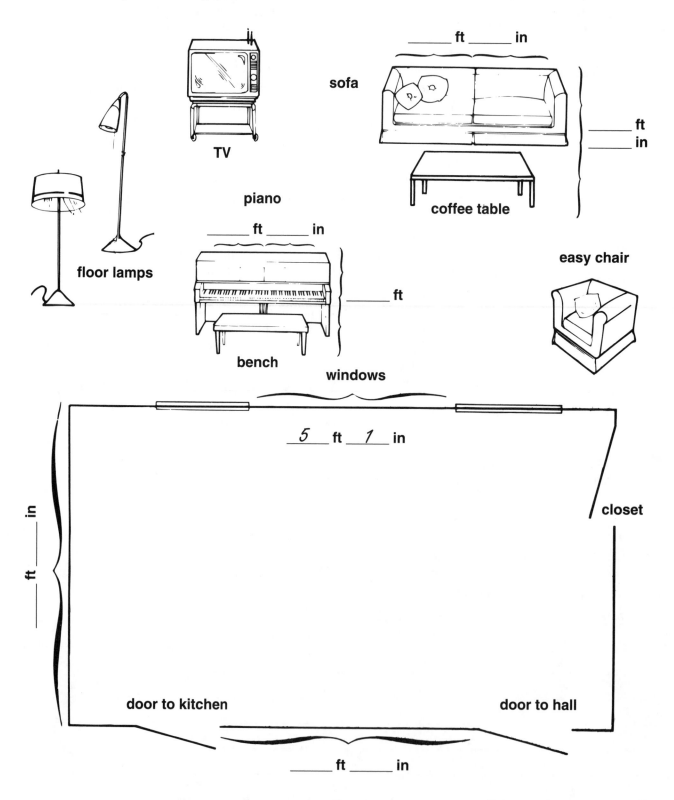

TV

floor lamps

piano

bench

sofa

_____ ft _____ in

_____ ft
_____ in

coffee table

easy chair

_____ ft _____ in

_____ ft

windows

_____5_____ ft ___1___ in

closet

door to kitchen

door to hall

_____ ft _____ in

ft _____ in

Lessons 23–24

1 ► **A fifty-year-old man is describing objects he remembers from his youth. Can you identify them?**

1. The first one I remember was like the one in that picture. It was made of wood, and it *was* heavy. Ours had only two dials, though: one for on-off and volume, and one to change stations. There was just one in the house, so my parents and my sister and I used to gather around it in the living room to listen to it.
   A radio.

2. We got our first one around 1950. Of course, it was only black and white, and there was only one channel. The screen was tiny in comparison to the ones we have today. I think it was nine inches. With all the tubes and everything, it weighed a ton.

   _____

3. There were a lot fewer brands than there are now, and they were all the same size—no kings, no 100's. No filters, either. And no choice of hard- or soft-pack. The choice was a lot simpler, but they were just as dangerous to your health.

   _____

4. They were a lot bigger and heavier, with only one speed. The tires (except during the war, when there was a rubber shortage) were bigger and heavier, too. When my father taught my sister to ride hers, he had her get on it like a boy. It was the only way he knew.

   _____

5. Ours was in the pantry, off the kitchen. It didn't have a freezer, and it was kept cold with ice, which was delivered to the house on a horse-drawn wagon. (That's how we got our fruits and vegetables, too.) You put a sign in the window telling the deliveryman how much you needed, so he'd carry the right amount into the house with his big metal tongs.

   _____

2 ► **Match the descriptions from a mail-order catalogue with the objects.**

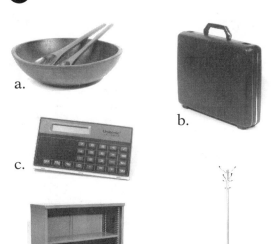

a.

b.

c.

d.

e.

_a_	1. [32] Wooden. 15" diameter. Holds 4 quarts. 2 lb
_____	2. [3] Durable plastic. Has inside pocket. Extremely strong and lightweight. 18" W x 3 1/2" D x 13" H; 5 lb
_____	3. [27] Aluminum. 50" high; 16 lb
_____	4. [1] Three shelves. 48" H x 11-7/8" D x 27-7/8" W; 75 lb
_____	5. [16] Thin design and credit card size. (3" x 2-1/4"); 1-3/4 oz

3 ▶ **Use the information in the picture to complete the conversation.**

A I was in a secondhand office furniture store today and saw a desk I'd like to get.

B Really? *Where would you put it?*

A _____ .

B In the bedroom! _____ ?

A Because it's the only place it'll fit, under the windows.

B _____ ?

A Sixty inches.

B _____ ?

A _____ .

B Whew! That's pretty big! _____ ?

A It's in pretty bad shape—I'd guess it's about fifty years old—but it's solid walnut.

[Illustration of a desk with measurements: 34", 60", 30"]

4 ▶ **Write a question and two answers for each item. Include comparisons in your answers.**

1. Scotia Square in Toronto is 68 stories. First Canadian Place is 72 stories.

   A *How high is Scotia Square in Toronto?*

   B *It's 68 stories high. It's 4 stories lower than First Canadian Place.*

   B *It's 68 stories high. First Canadian Place is 4 stories higher than Scotia Square.*

2. The biggest coral snakes are 48 inches. The biggest rattlesnakes are 96 inches.

   A _____

   B _____

   _____

   B _____

   _____

3. The largest land animals, adult African bull elephants, weigh about 8 tons. The largest mammals, adult blue whales, weigh about 150 tons.

   A _____

   B _____

   _____

   B _____

   _____

5 ▶ **The adjectives in these sentences are in the wrong order. Rewrite the sentences correctly.**

1. I'm going to throw away these English old two books.
   I'm going to throw away these two old English books.

2. You aren't going to wear your leather new brown jacket out in the rain, are you?

   _____

   _____

3. If I could afford it, I'd buy a Mercedes white air-conditioned.

   _____

   _____

4. Have you heard the opera Italian new exciting singer yet?

   _____

   _____

5. These handmade clay colorful tiles come from Mexico.

   _____

   _____

6 ▶ **Complete the chart with your own words.**

ORDER OF ADJECTIVES

	Ordinal number	Cardinal number	General	Age	Color	Material	Origin	Noun
a, an,			ugly	old	brown			shoe
the,								
this,								
these,								
etc.								

7 ▶ **Write sentences using words from your chart in exercise 6. Include at least two adjectives in each sentence. Use your imagination.**

1. _____

   _____

2. _____

   _____

3. _____

   _____

4. _____

   _____

5. _____

   _____

Lesson 25

▶ **Write an answer to this letter giving information about your apartment or house.**

Jean-Paul Fautier
231 Bourbon Street
New Orleans, L____

-2-

What a great idea to exchange apartments for the summer. I think you'll enjoy spending the summer here in New Orleans.

Let me tell you about my apartment. It's a small three-room apartment on Bourbon Street. The living room is 12 feet by 18 feet. The kitchen is large enough to eat in—about 10 feet by 12 feet—and the bedroom is about the same size. The apartment, which is in an old, historic building, has ceilings about 10 feet high, and there is a pleasant, iron-railed balcony about 4 feet wide just off the kitchen. I think you'll like it. It's in the middle of the old, historic French quarter. I look forward to hearing about your place.

Always,

Jean-Paul

_____

Dear Jean-Paul,

_____

_____

_____

_____

_____

_____

_____

_____

_____

_____ ,

_____

Lesson 26

1 ► For each personality trait, circle the number that you feel best applies to you. Numbers 1 and 5 represent opposite extremes.

Compared to others I know, I feel I am:						
usually a leader	1	2	3	4	5	usually a follower
careless	1	2	3	4	5	responsible
used to caring for others	1	2	3	4	5	used to being cared for by others
tense and inhibited	1	2	3	4	5	relaxed and sociable
unambitious	1	2	3	4	5	ambitious
very creative	1	2	3	4	5	not very creative
not good at persuasion	1	2	3	4	5	good at persuasion
seldom dependent on others	1	2	3	4	5	overdependent on others

2 ► Complete the sentences with either *over-* or *under-* plus one of the words in the box.

cook(ed)	price(d)	sell	supply
estimate(d)	ripe	slept	time

1. I wish I hadn't bought these bananas. They were _____*overpriced*_____ and

   they're _____ . I paid too much and I can't even use them yet.

2. I'm sorry about the steaks. I _____ how long they'd take so

   they're _____ . Next time I'll take them out sooner.

3. I'm late because I _____ , but I'll work

   _____ to make up for it.

4. Since we have an _____ of these parts, we'll have to

   _____ the competition in order to get rid of them.

Lesson 27

1 ▸ An interviewer asks eight people, "What do you remember best about growing up?" Before you listen to their responses, match the two parts of each sentence.

_c_ 1. Since my parents thought education was important,

_____ 2. I was the youngest of four children,

_____ 3. Everyone expected me to be lonely

_____ 4. My parents wanted us to develop our creativity;

_____ 5. I don't think my brother ever forgave me

_____ 6. I had to be very competitive

_____ 7. My older sister always stood up for me,

_____ 8. I didn't have any brothers or sisters.

a. because I was an only child.

b. therefore, we had very few toys—and no TV.

c. they pressured me to study a lot.

d. in order to keep up with my siblings.

e. so I had five "parents."

f. for being born.

g. As a result, I got away with a lot with my parents.

h. so I looked up to her a lot.

2 ▸ Now listen and complete the sentences using the statements from exercise 1. Make sure to change the pronouns.

1. The first person would probably say that *since her parents thought education was important, they pressured her to study a lot.*

2. The second person would probably say that _____

3. The third person would probably say that _____

4. The fourth person would probably say that _____

5. The fifth person would probably say that _____

6. The sixth person would probably say that _____

7. The seventh person would probably say that _____

8. The eighth person would probably say that _____

Lessons 28-29

1 ▶ **Before reading "Is the 'Only' Lonely?" mark an *X* next to the characteristics you think describe an only child.**

_____ selfish   _____ spoiled

_____ generous   _____ lonely

_____ intelligent   _____ unreliable

_____ ambitious   _____ able to get along with others

_____ creative   _____ looked down on by others

Is the 'Only' Lonely?

by Michael Jacobs

"You're an only child? That's too bad. You must have been very lonely without any sisters or brothers." "Everybody knows that only children are spoiled, so you must be used to having everything you want and getting your own way." "I should have expected you to be stingy, since you're an only child. They're not used to sharing."

In recent years, increasing attention has been paid to the matter of birth rank and its effect on personality, and properly so. Our development is unquestionably influenced by the number and nature of the people we grew up with. However, in the flood of studies on firstborns and later children, relatively little attention has been given to only children, or "onlies." As a result, powerful myths about onlies—that they are lonely, spoiled, and ungenerous—have continued to flourish. Thus, only children are regularly exposed to prejudiced reactions like the ones above.

Some apparently reputable sources have done little to drive away the myths. In 1900, E. W. Bohannon interviewed a group of teachers, asking them to describe onlies whom they had taught. He concluded that onlies were selfish, unhealthy, and often late to school. (Is it possible that the teachers thought first of students who had given them trouble?) In 1930, G. Stanley Hall (who trained thirty of the first fifty doctorates in psychology in the United States) said, "Being an only child is a disease in itself." *The Encyclopedia of Child Care and Guidance* remarks that "the only child need not be thought of as a complete tragedy." *Growing Pains*, published by the American Medical Association, says flatly, "The only child is a lonely child."

One problem with much of the research on birth rank is that it fails to differentiate firstborns and onlies. For example, the earliest birth-order researcher, Sir Francis Galton, reported in 1874 that firstborn and only children predominated among outstanding English scientists; however, he did not distinguish between the two groups. Robert C. Nichols studied 1,618 National Merit Scholarship finalists in 1964, reporting the percentage of firstborn winners from two- to six-child families. Nowhere does he mention onlies; yet it seems most unlikely that none would be among the group.

Nevertheless, there have been dozens of studies—in such countries as Russia, England, South Africa, the United States, India, and the Netherlands (the entire nineteen-year-old population)— of only children. These show that onlies are consistently more intelligent, creative, healthy and energetic, cooperative and dependable, looked up to, and well-adjusted than children with siblings.

From 1957 to 1968, *Time* magazine featured 36 women and 215 men on its covers. Of these, 7 of the women and 58 of the men were only children. Since 5 in 100 adults in the general population are onlies, their overrepresentation on *Time* covers is, respectively, 15% and 22%. On December 24, 1968, three Apollo astronauts reached the moon. All three were onlies. Recognizing this fact led someone to make another astonishing discovery: Of the first 23 astronauts in space, 21 were either firstborns or only children!

Can you guess what these people had in common? Hans Christian Andersen, Charles Pierre Baudelaire, Jean-Paul Sartre, Franklin and Eleanor Roosevelt, Leonardo da Vinci, Charles Lindbergh, Robert Louis Stevenson, Anna Magnani, Elvis Presley, Marilyn Monroe, and Sir Alec Guinness. You're right: *onliness.*

2 ▶ **Now answer these questions.**

1. Did your ideas about only children change as a result of reading the article? Why or why not?

_____

_____

2. If it is true that only children are more creative, dependable, and well-adjusted than children with siblings, why might this be?

_____

_____

3 ► Through the mail, Tommy received a book he hadn't ordered, with a letter from the publisher. Tommy returned the book, with another letter. Complete both letters with appropriate connectors. Some items have more than one answer.

Top Publisher's, Inc.

Dear Tommy:

_____ As/Since _____ our research shows that you are an avid reader of mysteries, we are sending you a copy of *Murder by Design* _____ your enjoyment. We know you didn't order the book, _____ of course there is no obligation on your part. _____, you may return the book if you wish.

2

Murder by Design is a sample of the Top Mystery of the Month series. _____ receive a Top Mystery each month, simply fill out the enclosed form. We accept all major credit cards _____ your purchase may be made easier.

Sincerely yours,

Walter Stevens

Walter Stevens
President, Top Publisher

Top Publisher's, Inc.:

Your research is wrong _____ I do not read mysteries _____ any reason. _____, I am returning the book.

Sincerely yours,
Tommy Jenkins
Tommy Jenkins

4 ► Write ten sentences or pairs of sentences, each with a different connector, using the following information.

Susan's parents couldn't pay her college expenses. She had to work and borrow.

1. *Susan had to work and borrow because her parents couldn't pay her college expenses.*

2. _____

3. _____

4. _____

5. _____

6. _____

7. _____

8. _____

9. _____

10. _____

5 ▶ **Complete each sentence with your own ideas.**

1. I wouldn't mind having some extra money so that _____ .

2. It's difficult to excuse people for _____ .

3. In order to _____ ,

   it's usually best to _____ .

4. You can often expect _____ ,

   since _____ .

5. I'm glad I _____ ,

   because as a result, I _____ .

6. I'm studying English to _____ .

   Therefore, _____ .

6 ▶ **Rewrite the paragraph below, changing each underlined part to a three-word verb from the box. Be sure to use correct verb forms.**

be in for	cut down on	get away with	keep out of	put up with
be up to	end up with	get out of	keep up with	run out of
catch up with	find out about	give in to	look down on	stand up for
come up with	get along with	go along with	look up to	walk in on

   I <u>didn't have any</u> cigarettes, so I went out to get some. Up ahead of me on the street, I saw my friend Scott, so I hurried to <u>meet</u> him. He asked me what I <u>was doing</u>, and when I told him, he said, "I used to smoke, too, because a lot of older kids I <u>admired</u> did, and I wanted to <u>be friends with</u> them. Then I developed a cough. When I went to the doctor for a checkup, he asked me why I smoked. Of course, I couldn't <u>give</u> any good reason. He told me that the other kids wouldn't <u>have a bad opinion of</u> me if I didn't smoke, and that I shouldn't be afraid to <u>defend</u> my own ideas if I didn't really want to smoke. He also said that if I didn't quit, I could <u>have</u> all kinds of problems and <u>expect</u> some real trouble. Well, I was scared, but not scared enough to quit; I'd always <u>surrender to</u> the urge to smoke. At first, I tried to <u>reduce</u> my smoking and <u>tolerate</u> the cough, the smell, the expense, and the danger to my health. Finally, I realized that you can't <u>do</u> it and <u>avoid</u> trouble, so I quit, cold. You'd better quit, too!"

I'd run out of cigarettes, so _____

_____

_____

_____

_____

_____

_____

_____

_____

_____

Lesson 30

▶ This memo is a response to a letter from the tenants of a building. Write the letter you think the tenants wrote.

MEMORANDUM

Clohr Properties 1010 Clairemont Street, Valley Stream, New York 11580

TO: The Tenants of 560 Taylor Place   **DATE:** July 15, 19—

FROM: Louis Garry, Office Manager   *LG*   **SUBJECT:** Complaints

    Thank you for your letter expressing your concern about a number of problems at 560 Taylor Place. I would like to inform you that I am doing something about them. A man has been hired to put out the garbage so that it does not collect in the hallways. A new lock has been installed on the front door so that strangers cannot get into the building and sleep in the lobby at night. Furthermore, a new intercom will be installed within the next month so that all the tenants can talk to visitors at the main door. I hope these measures result in less crime in the area.

_____

_____

_____

_____

_____

_____ :

_____

_____

_____

_____

_____

_____

_____

_____ ,

_____

Review of units 1-6

1 ▶ Complete the memo with the following connectors: *as, as a result, because, for, in order to, so that, therefore,* and *thus.* Some items have more than one answer.

MEMO

To: Christiana Johanson, Personnel
From: Gregor Yankov, President *GY*

_____*As/Because*_____ Valerie Landis has resigned, there is now a vacancy in Sales and Promotion. _____ fill the vacancy, I am moving Wilhelm Messler from Advertising, _____ his previous experience was in promotion. _____ , there will now be a vacancy in Advertising. _____ we can fill it as soon as possible, I would like you to recommend a candidate _____ the position who is already in the company.

---

2 ▶ Christiana Johanson and Gregor Yankov are meeting to discuss candidates for the opening in Advertising. Rewrite their conversation, combining each pair of sentences in brackets [ ] into one sentence.

A [We must name someone soon. It's essential.]
B [It should be someone with at least some experience in advertising. I recommend that.]
A I agree. Unfortunately, there aren't any people in the company with the right experience. Luis Aragon would have been suitable if he'd taken more courses. [He should do so. I've suggested it,] but he hasn't.
B [Then we'd better go to an employment agency. I recommend it.]

A *It's essential that we name someone soon.* _____

B _____

_____

A _____

_____

_____

B _____

_____

_____

3 ▸ **A photographer and his assistant are taking pictures for a newspaper ad for a furniture store. For each comment they make, write a sentence comparing dimensions.**

1. We can't use this mirror between these windows. The mirror is 24 inches wide. The space is only 22 inches wide.

   The mirror is two inches wider than the space between the windows. / The space between the windows is two inches narrower than the mirror.

2. We'll have to use different curtains on the windows, too. These are only 58 inches long, and the windows are 62 inches.

   _____

   _____

3. We can't put the 6-foot clock in that corner. The ceiling bends there, and it's too low, only 5 feet 8 inches. We'll have to use the clock in another shot.

   _____

   _____

4 ▸ **Now the photographer and his assistant are planning pictures for a mail-order catalogue. Rewrite their conversation, adding the adjectives in parentheses and putting them in the correct order.**

A I think these plates and those napkins would look great together. (plastic/shiny/red; Mexican/white/cotton)

B So do I. Should we put these bowls in the same picture? (hand-painted/Italian/three) Or would that be too much in one shot?

A Let's save the bowls for the picture with the set of place mats. (Philippine/four/grass) They go together better.

A *I think these shiny red plastic plates and those* _____

   _____

   _____

   _____

B _____

   _____

   _____

   _____

A _____

   _____

   _____

   _____

5 ▸ **Two salesclerks are talking about their work. Circle the correct choice in parentheses.**

A How do you like working here?

B I usually (find, imagine) it (enjoyable, enjoying) enough, but some of the other clerks (consider, watch) it pretty boring.

A But the customers can certainly (hear, make) you (getting made, mad), can't they?

B Yeah. Especially when they (call, watch) you stupid or incompetent when you've run out of merchandise and it isn't your fault.

A Do you think you'll (keep, make) (to work, working) here very long?

B Maybe a few more months. I can't (elect, see) myself (making, to make) a career of it—unless they (appoint, find) me (being president, president) of the company!

6 ▸ **Read about Mr. and Mrs. Brandt's worries. Then write what they hope and wish about the past.**

1. Mrs. Brandt drove to the supermarket alone, and she's late coming home. Mr. Brandt is afraid she was in an accident, and he's sorry he didn't go with her.

   Mr. Brandt hopes *Mrs. Brandt wasn't in an accident* .

   He wishes *he'd gone with her to the supermarket* .

2. Mrs. Brandt met a friend at the supermarket, but she couldn't stay and talk to her. She's worried that she hurt her friend's feelings when she said she had to go home.

   Mrs. Brandt hopes _____ .

   She wishes _____ .

3. When Mrs. Brandt gets home, she isn't sure she bought everything they need. She's sorry she didn't take a list.

   Mrs. Brandt hopes _____ .

   She wishes _____ .

4. When Mr. Brandt sees the groceries, he regrets all the more that Mrs. Brandt went to the store alone. He's concerned that she spent too much money.

   Mr. Brandt hopes _____ .

   He wishes all the more _____ .

7 ▸ **These sentences are from ideas expressed in the reading on page 67. Complete the sentences with *furthermore, moreover, however,* or *therefore*. Some items have more than one answer.**

1. We all want to be that lucky person who wins the lottery or who inherits money from an unknown relative. _____ , we cannot *make* such events happen.

2. We have no control over lucky events. _____ , the only way to make a difference in our luck is to control ourselves.

3. It is important to look for variety, new experiences. _____ , it is essential to be flexible.

4. Saying yes to uncertainty adds pleasure to life. _____ , it contributes to our luck.

5. Self-acceptance, courage, and action do not guarantee good luck. _____ , they do guarantee a richer and fuller life.

8 ▶ **A teenaged girl is complaining about her younger sister. Complete the sentences with one of these words:** *however, whatever, whenever, wherever, whichever,* **or** *whoever.*

Sometimes my little sister drives me crazy. She always wants to do _____*whatever*_____
I'm doing. _____ I go, she wants to go with me. _____ I'm
going out on a date, _____ I'm going out with, she wants to come along.
_____ I dress, she wants to wear the same thing. My mother will offer us
each a choice of two things. If I choose first, _____ the thing is, and
_____ one I choose, that's the one my sister is sure to want. I don't mind
sharing with her, but I don't want to share *everything*!

9 ▶ **These are comments that people make about their sisters and brothers. Complete each comment with one of the three-word verbs in the box. Make sure to use the correct forms of the verbs.**

be in for	come up with	get away with	keep up with
be up to	get along with	keep out of	look up to

1. I knew I _____*was in for*_____ trouble as soon as my brother was born,
   and my parents didn't pay any attention to me anymore.
2. My older sister and I _____ each other very well when growing
   up. We almost never disagreed.
3. Both of my older brothers were so good at everything that there was no way I could
   _____ them, no matter how hard I tried. But somehow I was
   never jealous of them. I've always _____ them for their
   accomplishments.
4. My little brother can't seem to _____ trouble. He
   _____ something all the time.
5. It seemed to me that when we were kids, I never _____
   anything. I always got caught. My brother and sister would do the same thing,
   _____ a good excuse, and not be punished.

10 ▶ **Give these people advice. Complete the conversations with your own ideas.**

1. **A** My younger sister is always borrowing my clothes. What can I do?
   B I suggest that you _____
   _____
   _____ .

2. **A** My younger son is very jealous of his brother and is always trying to start fights with him.
   I get angry with the younger one and feel sorry for the older one. What should I do?
   B I recommend that you _____
   _____ .
   It's necessary that your younger son _____
   _____ ,
   and that your older son _____
   _____ .

Lesson 31

1 ► Look at the reading on pages 70–71 of your textbook. Identify the main idea of each paragraph from the list below.

paragraph 2   a. In your own home, you can now do things with music that were never possible before.

_____ b. With interactive CD–ROMs, you can create your own video of a particular singer.

_____ c. Interactive rock will become more and more popular in the future.

_____ d. With interactive music, you can control different aspects of a song.

_____ e. This is what a CD–ROM is.

_____ f. At present, people can decide whether they just want to listen to music or whether they want to do things with the music.

_____ g. There is something new in the music busuness called "interactive rock."

_____ h. With interactive CD–ROMs, you can create your own band on your computer.

2 ► Place a stress mark (') over the correct syllable of each underlined word, according to whether it is a verb or a noun.

The Grass Lake City Council has announced that it will sign a <u>contract</u> with ABC <u>Research</u>, Inc., to <u>conduct</u> a <u>survey</u> of local homeowners. The <u>object</u> of the <u>research</u> will be to <u>record</u> opinions on recent changes in property values and taxes. The <u>survey</u> results from <u>protests</u> by Willard Wenk, of Ridge Road, who says, "This is an <u>insult</u>. How can the value of my property <u>decrease</u> while there's an <u>increase</u> in my taxes? I strongly <u>object</u> and <u>protest</u>!"

Lesson 32

1 ▶ Amanda and Benito are going to get married. Benito has never met Amanda's relatives, so Amanda is identifying them in pictures from her photograph album. Listen to Benito and Amanda's conversation. Then identify the people in each picture, reading from left to right.

her mother _____

_____

_____

_____   _____

_____   _____

_____   _____

_____   _____

Lessons 33-34

1 ▸ **Look at the pictures and your identifications in exercise 1 on the previous page. Write sentences using reduced restrictive clauses that describe the people in the pictures.**

1. *The little girl standing between Amanda's parents is her sister Arlene.*

2. _____

3. _____

4. _____

5. _____

6. _____

2 ▸ **First, combine each group of sentences into one sentence with two or more relative clauses. Next, rewrite the sentence with the clauses reduced. Finally, identify the thing described.**

1. It's a round Italian pie. It's made of dough, tomato sauce, and various toppings, and it's baked in an oven.

   a. *It's a round Italian pie that's made of dough, tomato sauce, and various toppings, and that's baked in an oven.*

   b. *It's a round Italian pie made of dough, tomato sauce, and various toppings, and baked in an oven.*

   What is it? *It's a pizza.*

2. It's a movie. It was produced by Steven Spielberg. It's about an extraterrestrial creature. He's left behind on Earth by his companions.

   a. _____

   b. _____

   What is it? _____

3. It's a famous structure. It's in Paris. It's made of iron, and it was built in 1889.

   a. _____

   b. _____

   What is it? _____

3 ▶ **All of these sentences contain relative clauses with pronoun subjects. Rewrite only those containing restrictive clauses that can be reduced. Do not rewrite the others.**

1. Did you hear about the robbery that was on the news last night?
2. Somebody robbed a store that's around the corner from where I live.
3. It's a store that sells appliances.
4. The person who robbed it took over $2,000.
5. The money that was stolen from the store was the day's receipts.
6. The police think it was an "inside job" that was done by someone who's working at the store.
7. The woman who's suspected and who's being sought by the police didn't show up at work today.
8. A man who was passing the store saw her come out of it at 11:00, long after she should have left.
9. She's someone who has worked there for seven years.
10. She's someone who's completely trusted by the owner and who's respected by the community.

Did you hear about the robbery on the news last night?

_____

_____

_____

_____

_____

_____

_____

_____

4 ▶ **What comes to your mind when you hear the word *lonely*? Write an answer of two or three sentences, using at least one reduced restrictive clause.**

_____

_____

_____

_____

_____

_____

_____

5 ▶ **Rewrite the conversations, combining the sentences in brackets [ ]
into one sentence and putting the adverbs and participial phrases
followed by a slash (/) in their correct position.**

1. **A** I can't find Larry! Have you seen him?

   B Sure. [right now/He's over there. He's playing with his friends.]

   A *I can't find Larry! Have you seen him?*

   B *Sure. He's over there right now, playing with his friends.*

2. **A** Did the plumbers call today?

   B Finally, at noon. [in the house/all morning/I stayed. I was waiting for their call.]

   A _____

   B _____

3. **A** Is Jorge coming?

   B He'd better be! [any minute/here/He's supposed to be. He's bringing our dinner.]

   A _____

   B _____

4. **A** Did you get your English homework done?

   B Yes. [all last night/hard/I worked on it. desperately/I was wishing I weren't taking English.]

   A _____

   B _____

6 ▶ **Read the sentences and answer the questions.**

1. Dora waited anxiously, hoping Elizabeth's train would come soon.
   Did Dora wait anxiously or hope anxiously? *She waited anxiously.*
2. Michiko sang happily, showing her joy at being alive.
   Did Michiko sing happily or show her joy happily? _____
3. Linda walked on, fast approaching her destination.
   Did Linda walk fast or approach her destination fast? _____
4. Julien talked to his friend, giving him some good advice.
   Who gave advice, Julien or his friend? _____

7 ▶ **Read the situation and answer the question. Someone gives you three boxes, one
containing two black stones, one containing two white stones, and one containing
a black stone and a white stone. The boxes, marked BB, WW, and BW, are labeled
to identify their contents, but the tops of the boxes are wrong. All of them are
labeled incorrectly. Your job is to take one stone at a time out of any box, without
looking inside. Using this process, or sampling, you are supposed to find out what
is inside all three boxes.**

   **What is the fewest number of stones you will need to remove in
   order to know what is inside each one?** _____

Lesson 35

▶ **Write a short newspaper review of a concert that you went to or a new compact disc that you heard recently.**

HENDERSON CONCERT A SELLOUT
by
Jason Myles

In case you've been out of touch, Rick Henderson gave a concert last night at the Velvet Arena. And in case you don't know who Rick Henderson is, well, he's the rock star who sings tunes about the working man. In fact, the song that is at the top of this week's list is his "On the Job." Henderson's concert was two hours of rock that had his unique magic about it. The people who play in his band deserve a lot of the credit for that magic, since they helped make the evening spirited and exciting. Don't miss Henderson and his band. They'll be at the Velvet Arena all this week.

_____

_____

_____

_____

_____

_____

_____

_____

_____

_____

_____

_____

_____

Lesson 36

1 ▶ **Refer to the reading on page 80 of your textbook. Are these the comments of an effective manager? Write *Yes* or *No*.**

No. 1. Your suggestion won't work. I know because we've tried it before.

_____ 2. You're supposed to be working on the budget, not sales. I'd appreciate it if you left sales to that department.

_____ 3. That's a very interesting idea. Let me think about it and get back to you.

_____ 4. May I remind you that I'm the boss here?

_____ 5. We all need to pull together if we're going to get this order out on time. I'd really appreciate your help on it, even though I know you're busy.

_____ 6. I called you all together because it's important that you know about this before you read it in the newspapers.

_____ 7. Please don't hesitate to come to me with your ideas, no matter how wild they may seem. The more creative they are, the more I'll welcome them.

2 ▶ **You are a manager, about to hire a new employee. The comments below are from applicants' references. First, complete each sentence with a word from the box. Then mark an *X* next to the characteristics you think are desirable for a good employee.**

self-centered	self-employed	self-starter
self-conscious	self-image	self-taught

_____ 1. He needed very little direction from me. He was very self-reliant, a

self-starter _____ .

_____ 2. He is very shy and _____ . He's self-critical and too aware of other's opinions to relax and be natural.

_____ 3. She is extremely insensitive to others because she is so _____ .

_____ 4. He is more concerned with his own _____ than with being a cooperative part of a working team.

_____ 5. After she left our company, she was _____ for several years, and she was very successful at working on her own.

_____ 6. He had almost no formal education. Although he is _____ , he can hold his own with any type of client.

Lesson 37

1 ► In each conversation you will hear a manager dealing with a situation. Is the manager's manner an example of effective communication? Write *Yes* or *No*.

Conversation 1 _Yes._

Conversation 2 _____

Conversation 3 _____

Conversation 4 _____

Conversation 5 _____

Conversation 6 _____

Conversation 7 _____

Conversation 8 _____

You've been coming in late, and we need you here on time.

RIGHT

2 ► Listen again to the conversations in exercise 1. Is the *first* speaker in each an employee or an employer? Check (✔) the correct column.

	Employee	Employer
Conversation 1	✔	_____
Conversation 2	_____	_____
Conversation 3	_____	_____
Conversation 4	_____	_____
Conversation 5	_____	_____
Conversation 6	_____	_____
Conversation 7	_____	_____
Conversation 8	_____	_____

3 ► Match each conversation with an appropriate ending.

_____ Conversation 1   a. I think it's important that I take the course, for my sake and the company's.

_____ Conversation 2   b. Please give it all your attention. It's crucial that it go out this afternoon.

_____ Conversation 3   c. It's essential that you be on time for your appointments.

_____ Conversation 4   d. I guess it's true that the more you get, the more you want.

_____ Conversation 5   e. Is it really necessary that he attend?

Lessons 38-39

1 ► Several people are discussing the advantages and disadvantages of watching television. These are some of the statements they make. Change each pair of sentences to one sentence, first with a subjunctive clause and then with an infinitive clause.

1. I want to relax at the end of the day by watching TV. It's important.
   a. *It's important that I relax at the end of the day by watching TV.*
   b. *It's important for me to relax at the end of the day by watching TV.*

2. My son has to stop watching so much TV, so he can develop his own imagination. It's essential.
   a. _____
   _____
   b. _____
   _____

3. My daughter has to take a computer course that they're presenting on TV, for college credit. It's necessary.
   a. _____
   _____
   b. _____
   _____

4. We all must keep up with world events, in order to understand other people. It's crucial.
   a. _____
   _____
   b. _____
   _____

2 ► Complete the sentences with your own ideas about how people could understand each other better.

1. It's important for everyone to _____
   _____.

2. I think it's urgent that _____
   _____.

3. It's crucial for us to _____
   _____.

4. It's necessary for everyone who wants to understand others to _____
   _____.

5. In my opinion, it's essential that people like me _____
   _____.

3 ► Use the ideas in each sentence to write a sentence with a double comparative.

1. Every time I see Monique, I enjoy her sense of humor more.
   The more I see Monique, the more I enjoy her sense of humor.

2. As I have more things to do, I get more efficient.

   _____

3. When I get angry, my voice gets quieter.

   _____

4. If you don't have very much, you can't lose very much.

   _____

5. Don't talk so much, and people will increasingly respect your opinion.

   _____

6. Keep practicing, and you'll improve your playing.

   _____

4 ► Complete the statements with your own ideas, using another comparative.

1. The more I study, _____

   _____.

2. The more I think about the world situation, _____

   _____.

3. The richer people are, _____

   _____.

4. I wish there weren't so many _____ people in the world. The fewer_____

   people there were, _____

   _____.

5. The less TV I watch, _____

   _____.

5 ► You need help working the new copying machine in your office. Ask for help in three different ways, according to who you're speaking to.

1. To an equal: _____

   _____

2. To a boss: _____

   _____

3. To an employee: _____

   _____

6 ▶ **Which of the people quoted here would agree with each of the comments below?**

EDUCATION

Educated people are as superior to uneducated ones as the living are to the dead.

Aristotle

Education is a social process.... Education is growth.... Education is not preparation for life; education is life itself.

John Dewey

Upon the education of the people of this country the fate of this country depends.

Benjamin Disraeli

Upon the subject of education, not presuming to dictate any plan or system respecting it, I can only say that I view it as the most important subject which we, as a people, can be engaged in....

Abraham Lincoln

A human being is not, in any proper sense, a human being until he is educated.

Horace Mann

Education does not mean teaching people what they do not know. It means teaching them to behave as they do not behave.... It is a painful, continual, and difficult work to be done by kindness, by watching, by warning, by precept, and by praise, but above all—by example.

John Ruskin

---

1. The more education we receive, the more human we become. *Horace Mann.*
2. The most crucial matter for us to be involved in is education. _____
3. It's essential for the future of our country that our people be educated. _____
4. The more you know, the more you grow. _____
5. It's most important that a teacher teach by example. _____

7 ▶ **A friend of yours wants to leave school. What reasons might he or she give for leaving? What reasons might you give for staying? Use words such as *necessary* and *crucial* and double comparatives in your arguments.**

I think I should leave school because:

it's necessary for me to get a job. _____

_____

_____

_____

I think you should stay in school because:

_____

_____

_____

_____

_____

Lesson 40

▶ **Write a memo about a problem at work or at school.**

MEMORANDUM
KLEIN STATIONERY

TO: Moira Klein
FROM: Josef Zenga

DATE: October 17
SUBJECT: Repairs

It is essential that we repair the roof in the northeast corner of the factory. Every time it rains, water leaks into the storage area and ruins some merchandise. The longer we wait, the more money the company loses. It is crucial that the company attend to this as soon as possible. Furthermore, it is essential that a good roofer do the job because we have had repeated problems with that roof. I think you will agree that it is urgent for us not to delay fixing it.

MEMORANDUM

TO: _____   DATE: _____

FROM: _____   SUBJECT: _____

_____

_____

_____

_____

_____

_____

_____

_____

_____

_____

_____

Lesson 41

1 ▶ **People who feel they have had good or bad luck made the statements below. Are they correct according to the reading on pages 90–91 of your textbook? Write *That's right* or *That's wrong*.**

That's right. _____ 1. I probably wouldn't be having such bad luck now if someone hadn't given me a black pearl.

_____ 2. If I hadn't gotten a sapphire for my birthday, I'll bet I wouldn't be as happy today.

_____ 3. It's a good thing I got that white mouse; I wouldn't be so lucky these days if I hadn't.

_____ 4. I should have consulted the dominoes on a Monday or a Friday instead of on a Wednesday. I'd be having better luck now.

_____ 5. I'm glad the coffee grounds took the shape of an elephant. If they'd formed thick, round blots, I could expect a lawsuit!

_____ 6. If my shoe hadn't landed with the toe up, I wouldn't be married today.

_____ 7. I wouldn't be having so much spiritual growth if I'd turned up the hanged-man tarot card.

2 ▶ **Fill in each blank with an article and a word ending in *-ist*.**

Someone who specializes in …

1. art is *an artist* _____ .

2. geology is _____ .

3. psychiatry is _____ .

Someone who …

4. plays the violin is _____ .

5. works on machines is _____ .

6. rides a motorcycle is _____ .

Someone who believes in …

7. individualism is _____ .

8. nationalism is _____ .

9. internationalism is _____ .

Lesson 42

1 ► Vito had conversations with five people at work. Before you listen, match the two parts of each sentence.

  _c_   1. If all goes well, by then

_____ 2. If I didn't like the job,

_____ 3. Yes, and I don't think I'd be so happy in my work now

_____ 4. I will have been working here for forty years

_____ 5. If I were interested in the job,

a. I wouldn't have stayed here this long.

b. if I hadn't learned to get along with my coworkers.

c. I will have saved enough money to retire.

d. I would have applied for it.

e. next September 1.

2 ► Each of Vito's conversations ended with a question. Listen and then choose the appropriate response for each question from the matched sentences in exercise 1 and write it below.

Conversation 1

Yes, and I don't think I'd be so happy in my work now if I hadn't learned to get along with my coworkers.

Conversation 2

_____

_____

Conversation 3

_____

_____

Conversation 4

_____

_____

Conversation 5

_____

_____

3 ► "The Roving Reporter" asks two teenagers about their plans. Listen and then complete the sentences below. You may use your own words.

Conversation 1 Lorna Genzel wants to:

a. *finish high school* _____ .

b. _____ .

c. _____ .

Conversation 2 Harry Lockwood hopes to:

a. _____ .

b. _____ .

c. _____ .

Lessons 43–44

1 ▶ **Refer to exercise 3 in Lesson 42 and complete the sentences.**

1. If Lorna Genzel does what she wants to do, in five years:

a. *she will have finished high school* _____ .

b. _____ .

c. _____ .

2. If Harry Lockwood does what he hopes to do, in five years:

a. _____ .

b. _____ .

c. _____ .

2 ▶ **Use the newspaper headlines to write sentences with *By* _____ , and the future perfect.**

1.
> September 5, 2008
> **SPACE PROBE REACHES PLANET NEPTUNE**

2.
> March 30, 2005
> **Automobile Company Produces 100 MPG Car**

3.
> February 2, 2006
> **ELECTRONICS FIRM INTRODUCES 3-D TV**

4.
> May 28, 2007
> **Doctors Discover Cancer Vaccine**

5.
> March 5, 2010
> **Robots Outnumber Human Workers**

1. *By 2008, a space probe will have reached the planet Neptune.* _____

2. _____

3. _____

4. _____

5. _____

3 ▶ **Use the information about Brian Brownell and the verbs in the box to write sentences with the future perfect and future perfect continuous.**

be	drive	know	live	see	smoke	study

Last year was an important one for Brian Brownell. He moved to Florida, met his future wife, got his driver's license, quit smoking, became an amateur radio operator, started studying Spanish, and stopped going to movies. If none of this changes, in four years Brian Brownell:

1. *will have lived/been living in Florida for five years.* _____

2. _____

3. _____

4. _____

5. _____

6. _____

7. _____

4 ► **Which statement is true? Choose *a* or *b*.**

SCIENTISTS HOPE FOR VACCINE AGAINST TWO MAJOR DISEASES

Scientists have found a way to separate the genes of the bacteria that cause tuberculosis and leprosy. As a result, they may be able to develop one vaccine that will work against both diseases.

"Although it will be some time before we can develop such a vaccine, we are hopeful that it can be done," said Dr. Rudolph Wozniak. "Separate vaccines for both TB and leprosy exist now, but both have major shortcomings."

TB affects about thirty million people worldwide. The present vaccine is effective in some parts of the world, but it is worthless in others, and no one is sure why. Ten to fifteen million people worldwide are affected by leprosy. A new vaccine seems to be effective, but it can be grown only in very small quantities.

The genes of all living things, including bacteria, contain directions for making proteins.

The human immune system identifies some of these proteins as "enemies"; it then produces antibodies that attack the proteins and kill the bacteria. In order to fight a disease, scientists make a vaccine from the bacteria that cause it, forcing the immune system to produce antibodies and so cure the disease.

This method of fighting disease has been known since 1796. However, newly gained knowledge about genes has allowed refinement of the process. Now that biologists are able to isolate specific genes, they are also able to combine them in new ways. Identifying and isolating the genes of TB- and leprosy-causing bacteria is a first, important step toward combining them into a single vaccine.

---

1. a. Genes contain bacteria.
   b. Bacteria contain genes.
2. a. Scientists have already developed a vaccine against both TB and leprosy.
   b. Scientists hope that they will soon develop a vaccine against both TB and leprosy.
3. a. If the present TB vaccine had been effective in all parts of the world, there would be no need for another.
   b. There would be a need for a new TB vaccine even if the present one had worked in all parts of the world.
4. a. We can assume that more people could have been cured of leprosy if the present vaccine could be produced in larger quantities.
   b. We can assume that more people could have been cured of leprosy if scientists knew more about its cause.
5. a. A vaccine against a disease consists of antibodies that will kill the bacteria causing it.
   b. A vaccine against a disease contains the bacteria that cause it.

5 ► **What does each statement imply? Choose *a* or *b*.**

1. If you hadn't gone to college, you wouldn't have such a good job now.
   a. You have a good job now even though you didn't go to college.
   b. You went to college, so you have a good job now.
2. He'd be a better doctor if he'd learned to be more sensitive toward people.
   a. He needs to be more sensitive toward other people in order to be a good doctor.
   b. He's a good doctor because he's so sensitive toward other people.
3. If they hadn't gone to work in the same company after finishing high school, they wouldn't have met, and they wouldn't be married now.
   a. They met at work.
   b. They met in high school.
4. If she liked studying, she would have gone on to college.
   a. She went to college.
   b. She didn't go to college.

6 ▶ **Two scientists are discussing some research they have just finished. Complete their conversation with the correct forms of the verbs in parentheses.**

A I think we've gotten pretty good results. What do you think?

B I _'d feel_ (feel) better if we _____ (get) a bigger sampling. There's never enough money available for research here. If there _____ (be), we _____ (be) able to hire someone to take a wider sample; our results _____ (be) more reliable.

A I think our results are reliable. If I _____ (not think) so, I _____ (not go ahead) and _____ (finish) the project. I _____ (suggest) that we stop halfway through and wait until there was either more time or more money.

B You're satisfied, then, and you think we should publish our results?

A Now I'm not so sure. I _____ (not have) any question if you _____ (not bring up) your doubts about the size of the sampling.

B We'd better think this over and not rush into anything.

A I agree. We'd both feel more secure.

7 ▶ **List three things you've done or haven't done in your life that you're happy about and three things that you're not happy about.**

I'm happy that I

1. _____ .
2. _____ .
3. _____ .

I'm not happy that I

4. _____ .
5. _____ .
6. _____ .

Now give reasons for being happy or unhappy, using mixed conditional sentences.

1. _____
2. _____
3. _____
4. _____
5. _____
6. _____

Lesson 45

► You have just received this letter from Al, a friend of yours. Answer the letter. You cannot visit Al in July because you have to go to summer school.

-2-

I'm really sorry to do this, but I have to ask you to change your visit from June to July. June will be a rather difficult time for me because of all the commitments I've already made which cannot be changed. If I'd planned ahead a little better, I wouldn't have to ask you to do this, but I hope you understand. At least, you'll have finished all your exams by July, and I will have arranged to take time off from work while you are here. Let me know as soon as possible if this change is O.K. with you.

Your friend,

Al

_____

_____ ,

_____

_____

_____

_____

_____

_____

_____

_____

_____

_____

_____

_____ ,

_____

Lesson 46

1 ▶ In each pair of sentences, *a* is based on "Spanish Prince of Song" on pages 100–101 of your textbook. Does *b* have approximately the same meaning? Write *Same* or *Different*.

_____*Same*_____ 1. a. His face is recognized everywhere, … (paragraph 1)
　　　　　　　　　b. Anyone who sees him knows who he is.

_____ 2. a. His songs appeal to people of all ages and cultures, from Japanese teenagers to Cuban grandmothers. (paragraph 1)
　　　　　　　　　b. Japanese teenagers like his songs more than Cuban grandmothers.

_____ 3. a. Underneath his natural humility, however, is a driving ambition and an obsession with meeting new challenges. (paragraph 2)
　　　　　　　　　b. He is not a humble person but someone who is very ambitious and who always needs a challenge.

_____ 4. a. … but during three years of intensive rehabilitation he went from wiggling his toes to crawling to walking with crutches, and finally to walking unaided. (paragraph 3)
　　　　　　　　　b. It took him a long time to learn to walk again.

_____ 5. a. Almost overnight, he went from being an unknown to being a star. (paragraph 5)
　　　　　　　　　b. After one performance one night, he became very famous.

_____ 6. a. This aspect of his career holds deep meaning for him. (paragraph 11)
　　　　　　　　　b. This part of his career is very important to him.

2 ▶ First, form nouns ending in *-cy* from the adjectives below. Then complete the conversation with appropriate nouns.

adequate *adequacy*	inaccurate _____
frequent _____	lenient _____
hesitant _____	secret _____

A mother is expressing to a friend her concerns about her son's behavior.

A I'm worried about Calvin. He's behaving with such _____*secrecy*_____ lately. He doesn't tell me anything, and he hates my questioning him. Sometimes I worry about my _____ as a mother.

B Oh, I'm sure you're a good mother. You may be treating him with too much _____ , though. Children not only *need* to be disciplined, but they really *want* to be. They need the feeling of security that rules can give them.

A I wouldn't say he's been lying to me exactly, but I have noticed some _____ in his stories about where he's been. And he's missing school with increasing _____ .

B Maybe you should see a counselor. You shouldn't have any _____ about asking for help, you know.

Lesson 47

1 ▶ **Read this questionnaire given to 110 secretaries at a convention. Then read the comments written by some of the secretaries. Write the letter(s) that gives an appropriate response to each question.**

Please write your comments.

1. Do you sometimes feel more intelligent than your boss?

   _____

2. What makes a good boss?

   _____

3. If you had a secretary, what would you have him or her do?

   _____

4. What part of your job, if any, would you like to see changed?

   _____

   _____

5. What do you enjoy most about your job?

   _____

6. How would life at the office change if you left?

   _____

   _____

a. I don't like being called a secretary. It's a stereotype because just the word gives people a certain impression. I'd change my title.

b. It wouldn't.

c. Sure. If you want a quick answer, ask the boss. If you want a right answer, ask the secretary.

d. Nothing. I'm sick and tired of doing jobs that anyone with half a brain could do.

e. She or he should be both patient and considerate, like mine.

f. Make all my appointments for me: doctor, lawyer, etc. I can't stand doing that for myself—and I even have to do it for my boss!

g. The salary.

h. A sympathetic, kind person, neither too busy nor too uninterested to listen.

i. No. She's a lawyer.

j. I'd appreciate being told more often when I've done a good job.

k. Not only would they have trouble replacing me, but they'd have to hire *two* people in my place.

l. That's one of my dreams! I'd enjoy someone else's doing for me all the things I don't like doing for myself, especially the filing.

1. ___c, i___   4. _____

2. _____   5. _____

3. _____   6. _____

 2 ▶ **Several of the secretaries who filled out the questionnaire were interviewed about their jobs. Listen to excerpts from the interviews. Then match the comments above to the secretary who you think wrote them.**

First secretary   ___c,_____

Second secretary   _____

Third secretary   _____

Fourth secretary   _____

Lessons 48-49

1 ▶ **Two people are talking about a staff meeting they've just left. Rewrite their conversation, changing the parts in brackets [ ] to sentences with possessive pronouns and active gerunds.**

A What did you think of the meeting?

B [It lasted for two hours! I didn't like that.] Caroline is a great boss in other ways, but [she lets Laverne talk all the time. I'm sick and tired of that.]

A I talked with Caroline about that once. [I told her. She said she appreciated that.] However, I don't notice any change.

B I told her the same thing. [We interfere in her business. Maybe she resents that.]

A [You want to help things run smoothly around here. She should be grateful for that.]

B You know what? I think so, too!

A *What did you think of the meeting?* _____

B *I didn't like its lasting for two hours!* _____

_____

_____

A _____

_____

B _____

_____

A _____

_____

B _____

2 ▶ **These are typical comments parents make when talking about their teenagers. Circle the correct form in parentheses.**

A Our teenagers can't stand (us, (our)) (criticize, criticizing) them.

B I don't blame them. Who likes (be, being) (criticize, criticized)?

A I know when I was young, I never wanted (to be, being) (tell, told) what I'd done wrong.

B But they're not used to (be, being) (tell, told) anything!

A True. Ours don't even like (us, our) (to tell, tell) them when they've done something well.

B No, they say they're tired of (our, us) (embarrassing, to embarrass) them!

3 ▶ **These are typical comments teenagers make when talking about their parents. Circle the correct form in parentheses.**

A My parents never want ((me,) my) (do, to do) anything.

B That's funny. My parents are just the opposite. I'm sick of (being, to be) (give, given) things to do.

A I mean anything that's *fun*. I'm used to (be, being) (tell, told) what to do, otherwise.

B Yeah, I wonder how our parents would like (our, us) (give, giving) them orders.

A They wouldn't want (to be, being) (boss, bossed) around, would they?

4 ▶ **Complete the sentences with your own ideas, using passive infinitives or gerunds. In some cases, both are possible.**

1. I like _____ .

2. I can't stand _____ .

3. I don't usually mind _____ .

4. I hate _____ .

5. I'm not used to _____ .

6. I appreciate _____ .

5 ▶ **Two roommates are having a disagreement. Rewrite their conversation, changing the parts in brackets [ ] to sentences with *either … or, neither … nor,* or *not only … but (also).***

A [We have to talk. If not, then we're going to have some real problems.]

B I agree. I've been wanting to talk to you, but [I've been afraid. If not, then I've been embarrassed.] Do you want to go first?

A Sure. Here's what bothers me most. [I'm tired of paying more than my share of the rent. What's more, I can't afford to keep it up.]

B You're right. I'm sorry. [But lately I've been out of work. If not, then I've just had part-time jobs.]

A I know. [You're not stupid, and you're not lazy.] What seems to be the problem?

B [I seem to be overqualified for everything. If not, then I'm underqualified.]

A [Well, I hope you find work soon. What's more, I hope you're able to pay what you owe.]

A *We either have to talk, or we're going to have some real problems.* _____

B _____

_____

A _____

_____

_____

B _____

_____

A _____

B _____

A _____

_____

6 ▸ **Imagine that you're giving someone advice about handling criticism. Using the information in the magazine article, write recommendations with** *either ... or, neither ... nor,* **and** *not only ... but (also).*

How to React to Criticism

Many of us react badly to criticism of our work because we see it as both a comment on what we have *done* and an evaluation of what we *are*. "When one of the doctors criticizes me, I get defensive," says Viola, a nurse. "I feel like a child again, being scolded, and I want to explain that it isn't my fault."

This is a common response, but a destructive one. There are more constructive ways of handling criticism.

1. Try to be objective. When Sol was criticized by his new employer for not having made a sale, Sol's reaction was to feel sorry for himself. "I had put everything I had into making that sale," Sol says," and I felt that I had failed as a person. I had to learn through experience not to react emotionally to each setback, not to confuse my *self* with my *work*."

2. Take time to cool down. Rather than responding immediately to criticism, take some time to think over what was said. Your first question should be whether the criticism is fair from the other person's point of view. The problem may be a simple misunderstanding of what you did or your reasons for doing it.

3. Take positive action. After you cool down, consider what you can do about the situation. The best answer may be "nothing." "I finally realized that my boss was having personal problems and taking them out on me because I was there," says Sheila. "His complaints didn't really have anything to do with my work, so nothing I said or did was going to change them." In Sheila's case, the best solution was to quit her job. However, that's an unusual and extreme solution. You may request a conference and ask for more information. You may simply explain your point of view without expecting a response or an in-depth discussion. You may even decide that the battle isn't worth fighting this time. The key, in any case, is to have a rational plan.

4. Don't be afraid to admit your mistake. If you decide that the criticism was justified, the best response is to admit it. But don't overdo your apology. The result will be to make the other person, if angry, even angrier and more uncomfortable. You may want to explain what you're doing to correct the situation and ask for any other suggestions.

5. Don't overdo self-criticism. Many of us believe that if we criticize ourselves first, we'll diminish our chances of being criticized. But this too is a destructive attitude, for it prevents our learning from our mistakes and moving forward.

If there are constructive ways of receiving criticism, there are also constructive ways of giving it. "The first time I had to criticize a secretary for coming in late, I couldn't think of a tactful approach," says Rodolfo. "Luckily, a more experienced coworker had some good advice. She told me to concentrate on the problem, not the person. So I went to the secretary and asked her, 'What can we do about this?' And she came up with the solution! She decided to take an earlier bus, and she was never late again."

1. *It is an overreaction to see criticism as not only a comment on what we have done but also an evaluation of what we are.*

2. _____

3. _____

4. _____

5. _____

6. _____

Lesson 50

▶ Write a letter complaining about something you are tired of on radio, on television, or in the newspaper.

Mr. Daniel Sykes, Station Manager
Station KRDTV
600 Ferrier Street
Seattle, Washington 98115

Dear Mr. Sykes:

Last night I watched Jan Rover on <u>Nightshow</u>. I'm getting a little tired of her making fun of other people. She not only likes to be teased herself, but she also loves to tease other people. However, some people don't like it, and she should respect that. For example, I'm sure many celebrities are tired of being teased about their appearance by Jan Rover.

I've never gotten used to Miss Rover's telling dirty jokes on television when millions of people are watching. Furthermore, I really don't like her making fun of the things that I respect. She should either calm down or stop appearing on television.

Sincerely,

Herbie Quigley
Herbie Quigley

_____ ,

_____

_____

_____

_____

_____

_____

_____

_____

_____

_____

_____

_____ ,

_____

Lesson 51

1 ▶ Refer to the reading and illustration on pages 110–111 of your textbook.
Match the items that are most closely associated.

_e_ 1. morgue

_____ 2. autopsy

_____ 3. bullet

_____ 4. DNA

_____ 5. print

_____ 6. crime

_____ 7. knife

_____ 8. lymph nodes, bile

a. medical examination

b. ballistics

c. gall bladder

d. stab wound

e. building

f. murder

g. genetic material found in blood, skin, or hair sample

h. foot, finger

2 ▶ Complete the paragraphs below, using words from the list in the box.

cheerful	harmful	painful	tearful
cheerless	harmless	painless	tearless
doubtful	hopeful	powerful	thoughtful
doubtless	hopeless	powerless	thoughtless

"Police," I said when she came to the door. Her husband had died of a ___*powerful*___

dose of poison the day before. It was my job to find his killer. His widow was surprisingly

_____ ; her eyes were _____ . "Come in!" she said, smiling.

We sat. "At least his death was _____," I said. "He felt nothing." She gave me

_____ a look.

"I did it," she cried abruptly. "I thought it was a _____ sleeping pill." So

the case was already solved? Somehow, I was _____ . Confessions don't usually

come so soon or so easily, and I hadn't been _____ that this one would.

Something was wrong....

Lesson 52

🔊 **1** ▶ **Listen to the clues and fill in the blanks.**

1. There are _____*five*_____ houses on Maple Street.

2. The person who lives in the _____ house is an _____ .

3. Mr. and Mrs. Goren, who are both _____ and who live in the _____ house, own a dog. They're the only couple who live in the neighborhood.

4. The person living in the _____ house, which is the one on the _____ , drinks milk.

5. Alma, who is a _____ , drinks soda. She lives in the _____ house.

6. The blue house is _____ the yellow house and the red house. The _____ house is the middle house on the street.

7. The person whose hobby is _____ and whose pet is a bird is an _____ .

8. The _____ lives in the _____ house.

9. The people whose hobby is making _____ drink _____ .

10. The _____ , who drinks _____ , enjoys _____ .

11. The _____ likes to _____ .

12. The person who has a snake for a pet likes _____ and lives next to the person whose pet is a cat.

2 ▶ **Fill in this chart, using the information in exercise 1. Each person or couple has one house, a different occupation, one hobby, one pet, and a different choice of drink. Hint: You might want to begin with the colors of the houses.**

color of house					
occupation			*artist*		
hobby					
pet					
drink					

What's the hobby of the person who drinks water? _____

What color is the house of the person whose pet is a fish? _____

Lessons 53–54

1 ▶ **Match the items.**

_g_ 1. It seems to me you should call the police.

_____ 2. Are you going to work today?

_____ 3. Did you make that phone call?

_____ 4. Is it 9:00 yet?

_____ 5. Where are your keys? Do you suppose you left them in the car?

_____ 6. I hope the meeting doesn't last very long.

_____ 7. I thought I'd mailed this letter days ago.

a. I might or I might not. I haven't decided.

b. It must be by now.

c. You must not have.

d. I must have.

e. It shouldn't.

f. I couldn't. I didn't have a chance.

g. O.K., I will.

2 ▶ **Two people are just arriving home from a vacation. Complete their conversation, choosing the correct modal auxiliary in parentheses for each blank.**

A I'm glad to be getting home. You _____ _must be_ _____ (must, (must be), must have), too.

B Are you saying that because I lost our traveler's checks? I wish you hadn't reminded me.

A I _____ (shouldn't, shouldn't be, shouldn't have). I'm sorry. Try to forget about it.

B I wish I _____ (could, could have, could be) , but I _____ (can't, couldn't, couldn't have). We were lucky we didn't have trouble getting them replaced.

A We certainly _____ (can, could have had, could). Ah, there's the house, at last. Look! The garage door is open! Do you suppose we left it that way?

B It seems unlikely that we _____ (must have, would have, could have been), but we _____ (must have, would have, could have been). Unless … Is there any possibility that someone's broken in?

A Somebody _____ (might, might have, might be). You stay here. I'll go and check.

B You _____ (couldn't, might not, shouldn't). What if someone's still here?

A You're right. We'd better go next door and call the police.

3 ▶ **Complete each conversation with a speculation. Include modal auxiliaries.**

1. **A** A strange thing happened today. A package came addressed to me, but without any return address. Inside was a book I've been wanting, which I didn't order.

   B _____

   _____

   A _____

   _____

2. **A** I think we're lost. I was sure we were following the directions that May gave us.

   B _____

   _____

   A _____

   _____

4 ► **Can you solve these mysteries? Most of the clues are contained in the stories. The solutions follow exercise 6.**

DEATH ON THE SLOPES

Al Gardner, who is a travel agent in Chicago, sells a man two different types of airplane tickets for Switzerland. A week later he reads a newspaper article about a skiing accident in Switzerland, in which an American woman has died. According to the article, the woman's husband, who is overcome with grief, says that he was already at the bottom of the slope when he looked up and saw her fall. Gardner recognizes the husband's name; it is the man to whom he had sold the two tickets a week earlier. He knows immediately that the husband is lying and has murdered his wife. The man never intended for his wife to return to Chicago alive.

How does Gardner know that the man is a murderer?

THE CASE OF THE MISSING CHECK

Peter Lauridsen, who is a member of a law firm, called the police and told them that a check for $10,000, which could be cashed by anyone, had been stolen from his office. He said that he had hidden the check in a law book, and he believed that his secretary had seen him do this and had stolen it. The check had been between pages 137 and 138 of *The U.S. Criminal Code*.

Just as the police arrived at Lauridsen's building to investigate the theft, there was a crash. The secretary had fallen out of a window and had been killed. In his pocket the police found a note that said: *"Criminal Code—between pages 137 and 138."* However, they didn't find the check.

One of the police officers suggested that they look for the book and the check in Lauridsen's office. But another, whose mind worked more quickly, said, "There's no way a check could be between those pages. It's impossible. I think Lauridsen planned the whole thing. But he made one bad mistake."

When the officers questioned Lauridsen, he soon confessed that he was the one who had cashed the check, tried to put the blame on his secretary, and then murdered him.

How did the second officer know that nothing could be hidden between those two pages?

---

5 ► **Add relative pronouns and any necessary commas. In some cases, there is more than one possible answer. Then solve the mystery. The solution follows exercise 6.**

THE DANGEROUS DREAM

Randall Ming owns a factory ___*that*___ produces auto parts _____ are shipped all over the country. One of his employees is a man named Henry Porter _____ has worked for Mr. Ming for many years. Porter _____ is a night security guard works every weeknight from 11:00 P.M. to 7:00 A.M. He also acts as Mr. Ming's chauffeur. One Thursday morning at 7:30, Porter arrives at Mr. Ming's house _____ is just outside the city in _____ his factory is located. Porter is to drive Mr. Ming _____ is taking a business trip to the train station.

"I wish you wouldn't take this trip," Porter tells Mr. Ming. "Last night, just after midnight, I had a dream _____ was very realistic in _____ you got killed in a train wreck."

Mr. Ming _____ immediately becomes very angry doesn't thank Porter for the warning _____ he has given him. Instead he says, "You, a man _____ I trusted! You're fired!"

Why does Mr. Ming fire Porter?

---

6 ► **Rewrite the paragraphs, combining each pair of sentences in brackets [ ] into one sentence with either a nonrestrictive or a restrictive relative clause.**

[Sherlock Holmes is probably the most famous detective in literature. He was created by Sir Arthur Conan Doyle.] [Doyle wrote sixty novels and short stories about Holmes. Doyle lived from 1859 to 1930.]

[*A Study in Scarlet* was Doyle's first novel about Holmes. *A Study in Scarlet* also introduced Holmes's faithful friend, Dr. Watson.] [The book begins with Watson's being wounded in a war. The war was being fought in Asia.] [Watson is sent home to London with a small pension. It is hardly enough to pay his bills at the inexpensive hotel where he takes a room.] [By chance he meets Stamford. Stamford is an old friend, and Watson tells him about his difficulties.] [Stamford tells Watson about Sherlock Holmes. Holmes is an amateur detective.] [Holmes lives at 221B Baker Street. He is looking for someone to share his rooms.] [The two men meet, and Watson decides to move in with Holmes. He likes him immediately.]

[Watson found Holmes to be an amazingly contradictory man. He knew nothing about literature and philosophy, but he knew everything about chemistry, anatomy, and crime.] [Holmes found Watson to be a person of average intelligence. Watson nevertheless helped him solve the long series of crimes in which the two became involved.] [In spite of their differences, the two men formed a friendship and a partnership. It lasted for 43 years, untilthe death of Arthur Conan Doyle, their creator, in 1930.]

Sherlock Holmes, who was created by Sir Arthur Conan Doyle, is probably the most famous detective in literature.

_____

_____

_____

_____

_____

_____

_____

_____

_____

_____

_____

Solutions for exercise 4

"Death on the Slopes" One of the airplane tickets was for a round trip, but the other, which was for the man's wife, was only a one-way ticket.

"The Case of the Missing Check" In books published in the United States, the pages that are on the right have odd numbers, such as 137. The pages that are on the left have even numbers, such as 138. Since the two pages would be back to back, nothing could be hidden between them.

Solution for exercise 5

"The Dangerous Dream" As a night security guard who was supposed to be working between 11:00 P.M. and 7:00 A.M., Porte shouldn't have been asleep and dreaming just after midnight. He wasn't doing his job.

Lesson 55

▶ **Write Sergeant Blaine's report of her investigation.**

Sgt. Blaine I'm Sgt. Blaine, and I'd like to ask you a few questions about the Allan Street burglaries, which I'm investigating.

Mr. Fidich Sure, but I'm a sound sleeper. I never hear anything.

Sgt. Blaine But the last time the burglar left by the fire escape—right by your window. And you heard nothing? You must have!

Mr. Fidich Listen, Officer, I don't want to get involved, but it seems to me that you should question that Miss Renzo, who I think is very suspicious.

Sgt. Blaine Why do you say that?

Mr. Fidich Well, no one knows anything about her, and the burglaries only started after she moved in.

Sgt. Blaine So you think she could have had something to do with them?

Mr. Fidich She could have, but don't let her know I told you so.

Granville Police Department
88th Precinct

_____

_____

_____

_____

_____

_____

_____

_____

_____

_____

_____

Lesson 56

1 ▶ **The statements below are based on the reading on pages 120-121 of your textbook. Which are facts and which represent the writer's opinions? Write *Fact* or *Opinion*.**

_Opinion_____ 1. Martha Graham is practically a synonym for modern dance.

_____ 2. Graham has been called one of the greatest artists the United States has ever produced.

_____ 3. In the early 1920s, Graham began to feel the need for a new and different style of dance.

_____ 4. Graham's early dances of the 1930s were stark and simple; during the 1940s–1960s, they became more complex.

_____ 5. Graham's dances can be interpreted in many different ways.

_____ 6. The theme of rebirth is evident in the dramatic series of falls to the floor that Graham invented.

_____ 7. Martha Graham's influence will survive long after her death.

_____ 8. The Martha Graham Dance Company continues to tour the United States and the world, even after her death.

_____ 9. What will make Graham's work last is her successful mixing of themes.

_____ 10. Graham's message is for everyone, yet her work is individual.

2 ▶ **All of the words in the box are related to words in the reading about Martha Graham. Choose one for each synonym or definition below.**

admirable	attractive	illustrative	memorable
alternative	breakable	informative	unbelievable
applicable	distinctive	inventive	unthinkable

_attractive_____ 1. good-looking

_____ 2. appropriate

_____ 3. fragile

_____ 4. telling you what you want to know

_____ 5. used as an example

_____ 6. incredible

_____ 7. unlike any other

_____ 8. worth looking up to

_____ 9. unforgettable

_____ 10. having innovative ideas, creative

Lesson 57

1 ▶ **Listen to the conversations between people who have attended various events. Write the number of each conversation under the appropriate illustration.**

Mirrors

A musical based
on the poems of

INGRID KAYE

a. Conversation _____

HOCKEY
Jefferson Square
Garden

LESLIE
vs.
MARSHFIELD

8:00
P.M.

★

$6.00

Friday, October 4

...FIELD $6.00

b. Conversation _____

THE CAST

Romeo ..... Ved Singh
Juliet ..... Sonia Orlovsky

c. Conversation _____

Palace
Performing Arts
Center

Pilobolus Dance
Theater

Thurs., Oct. 3 8:00 P.M.

$14.50

8:00 P.M.

d. Conversation _____

Belson
Jazz Society

presents

Betty Foster

The greatest of all jazz singers

Sunday, October 6
8:00 P.M.
Info. 555-6688

e. Conversation _____

M.S. Gallery   Paintings by
Horst Ten Eyck, Monday–
Saturday 10:00 A.M. to 5:00
P.M., ends October 22. Outdoor
sculpture by Robert Boden,
through November.

f. Conversation _____

2 ▶ **Write *That's right* or *That's wrong* for each statement. Listen to the conversations in exercise 1 again if necessary.**

_____*That's right.*_____ 1. The person who didn't care for *Mirrors* would have preferred seeing a murder mystery.

_____ 2. The person who wasn't crazy about the hockey game would rather have gone to a football game.

_____ 3. The person who didn't like *Romeo and Juliet* would have liked a different kind of play by Shakespeare more.

_____ 4. The person who didn't care for Pilobolus would have preferred classical ballet.

_____ 5. Classical music is what the person who didn't enjoy jazz would rather have heard.

_____ 6. More abstract, nonrepresentational art is what the person who didn't care for the gallery exhibit would have preferred.

3 ▶ **Listen to the questions and responses. Are the responses tactful? Write *Yes* or *No*.**

1. _____   2. _____   3. _____   4. _____

Lessons 58-59

1 ▶ **Rewrite the conversation, changing each sentence in brackets [ ] in either of the two possible ways, to give it more emphasis.**

A [I'd like to do something different this weekend.] How about going camping?

B Sounds good. [I'd really like to do some fishing,] and we could combine the two. Where shall we go? Up to Ford Lake?

A [I'd rather go to the Senegee River.] There are fewer bugs and not as many people. Do you want to invite anyone else?

B [I'd like to see my brother go.] He's only gone fishing a couple of times. [He needs more experience.]

A *What I'd like to do this weekend is something different.*
   Something different is what I'd like to do this weekend.

B _____

_____

A _____

_____

B _____

_____

2 ▶ **Give your true opinion.**

1. If you had a choice of going camping or going fishing, which would you rather do?

_____

2. If you had a choice of going to the mountains or to the seashore, where would you prefer to go?

_____

3. If you had a choice of hearing Placido Domingo or Prince, who would you rather hear?

_____

3 ▶ **Friends of yours invite you to do the things you did *not* choose in exercise 2. Complete their invitations and respond tactfully with your true preferences.**

1. **A** How would like to go _____ this weekend?
   B _____

_____

_____

2. **A** Let's go to the _____ for our vacation this year, O.K.?
   B _____

_____

_____

3. **A** I'd like to go hear _____ next month. Would you like to go?
   B _____

_____

4 ▶ **Read the following movie reviews.**

MOVIES AROUND TOWN

Bach — The life of the great composer, Johann Sebastian, as seen through the eyes of his youngest son, Johann Christian. Despite fine performances of Bach's incomparable music, the truly terrible acting makes this a "don't bother" film. Wait for the soundtrack recording.

Behind the Times — A young couple is carried by time machine back to the Civil War, where they discover that their respective ancestors were on opposite sides. The idea is promising. The result, however, fails to live up to the idea.

Germ — While the director's previous science fiction movie, *Wasp Attack*, had moments of high excitement and almost unbearable suspense, this effort has none. The human actors plod their way through the boring story, whereas the germ has all the good lines.

I Love It — Hilarious romantic comedy starring that real-life couple, Lena Desmond and Berkeley Stoddard. Sparkles with wit and understanding of the human condition in spite of occasionally heavy-handed direction and some lazy editing.

Lost — Heartbreaking story of a boy who wanders away from his family during a camping trip in the mountains. This is the first movie for Christopher Ryan, who plays the boy. Nevertheless, his performance is entirely affecting. Bring your handkerchiefs.

Murder at Eight — Not a whodunit, since we know from the beginning who the murderer is, yet a suspense-filled psychological tale that never lets up on the surprises. Superb performance by the always-watchable Alexandra Yasmine.

Shall We Dance? — Bartók's ballet *The Wooden Prince* translated to the silver screen. In spite of Nicholas Gorsky's athleticism and the beautiful photography, the ballet should have remained on stage.

Still Waters — Updated Western about a family's search for a new life on the western plains and the hardships they face. Marta Linz is miscast as the mother. Nonetheless, well worth seeing for the other actors' performances, the stunning photography, and the fast-moving story.

Now complete each sentence with *liked* or *didn't like*, according to the opinions expressed in the movie reviews.

The reviewer ...

1. _____*liked*_____ the music in *Bach*, whereas she _____ the acting.

2. _____ the idea of *Behind the Times*, while she _____ the result.

3. _____ *Wasp Attack*, yet _____ *Germ*.

4. _____ the acting in *I Love It*. Nevertheless, she _____ the direction and editing.

5. _____ the acting of Christopher Ryan in *Lost* despite its being the boy's first movie.

6. _____ Alexandra Yasmine's performance in *Murder at Eight*.

7. _____ *Shall We Dance?* Nonetheless, she _____ the photography.

8. _____ Marta Linz's performance as the mother in *Still Waters*. On the other hand, she _____ the photography and the story.

5 ▶ **Give your true opinion.**

1. Which of the movies reviewed above do you think you would like the most? Why?

_____

_____

2. Which of the eight movies do you think you would like the least? Why?

_____

_____

6 ▶ Complete the conversations with tactful responses.

1. **A** I don't see how you can like Bergman's movies. I think they're dull and depressing.
   B *You might like them, too, once you've gotten used to them.*

2. **A** Do you really like modern furniture? I find it too plain and uncomfortable.
   B _____

3. **A** You actually like jazz? How can you?
   B _____

4. **A** How can you eat that hot, spicy food?
   B _____

5. **A** Did you say you're going to a poetry reading Wednesday? I can't imagine anything more boring.
   B _____

7 ▶ Rewrite the conversation, changing each *but* to a different connector and making any other necessary changes.

A How was your day?
B It started out O.K., but it didn't end very well. I got fired.
A Fired! What happened?
B Mr. Delon said he had to let me go, but I'd been doing good work. In a way, I wasn't surprised, but it was still a shock. I knew I was doing O.K., but the company's been losing money.
A You'd indicated that, but I didn't realize your job was in danger. You may have lost this job, but you shouldn't have any trouble getting another one.
B I hope not, but I still don't look forward to job hunting again. It's no fun, but maybe I'll get an even better job this time.

A *How was your day?*
B *In spite of starting out O.K., it didn't end very well. I got fired.*
A _____
B _____
_____
_____
A _____
_____
_____
B _____
_____

Lesson 60

▶ **Write a tactful letter in which you do not accept an invitation.**

Dear Joshua,

   I really appreciate the invitation to go with you to see
the Philip Glass opera. I like classical opera, but, as you know,
Philip Glass is a contemporary composer. I find his operas long
and unexciting despite the good reviews they have
received. His music, which I like to listen to when I meditate,
is not what I'd prefer to listen to while sitting for four hours.
<u>Aïda</u> is what I would like to see. I have tickets for next
month for the two of us.

                                        As ever,
                                        Karen

_____ ,

_____

_____

_____

_____

_____

_____

_____

_____

_____

_____

_____

_____

_____

                                _____ ,

                                _____

Review of units 7-12

1 ▶ Tony Lombardo is being forced to retire from his job at the age of 72. This is a letter he wrote to his employers, asking them to reconsider. Complete the letter, using the connectors in the box. Some items have more than one answer.

despite	in spite of	nonetheless	whereas	yet
however	nevertheless	on the other hand	while	

Dear Mr. and Mrs. Field:

I want to protest my being forced to retire _____*despite/in spite of*_____ the fact that I am both able and willing to continue working.

You know that I do a full day's work _____ my age. _____ , there are other workers at the plant who are half my age, do <u>not</u> do a full day's work; _____ , they are not being asked to leave.

_____ I understand that the law says I will be unable to work full time at 72, I cannot, _____ , understand why you want to keep me from working part time.

Please reconsider your decision.

Sincerely yours,

Tony Lombardo
Tony Lombardo

2 ▶ Use the ideas in the paragraphs to write sentences in the future perfect or future perfect continuous.

Mr. Lombardo started working for the Field Company when he was 22. He's had seven different positions with the company. This is the third generation of the Field family he's worked for.

Mr. and Mrs. Lombardo were married when Mr. Lombardo was 22. They've lived at three different addresses. They began living at their present home seven years after their marriage. They've seen a lot of changes in their neighborhood.

By the time Mr. Lombardo retires at 72:

1. *he will have worked/ been working for the Field Company for 50 years.*

2. _____

3. _____

Soon Mr. and Mrs. Lombardo will have been married for 50 years. By then:

4. _____

5. _____

6. _____

3 ► Rewrite points 1–4 in the ad from City National Bank, using *either ... or*, *neither ... nor*, or *not only ... but (also)*.

1. *We're not only the largest bank in town, but also we're offering the highest interest rates on your savings.*

2. _____
   _____
   _____
   _____

3. _____
   _____
   _____
   _____

4. _____
   _____
   _____
   _____

CITY NATIONAL BANK

Why should you do
your banking with us?

Because:

1. We're the largest bank in town, and we're offering the highest interest rates on your savings.
2. You can choose our ordinary savings rate. If not, you can choose our extraordinary rate ($1,000 minimum deposit).
3. We give you the highest interest rates, and we give you the lowest rates on loans.
4. We're not too large to know you personally. What's more, we're not too small to give you full service.

---

4 ► Rewrite each sentence as a mixed contrary-to-fact conditional.

1. Ibrahim's not ambitious, so he hasn't looked for a higher-paying job.
   If Ibrahim were ambitious, he would have looked for a higher-paying job.
   _____

2. He's so absent-minded that he even forgot to apply for a promotion he might have gotten.
   _____
   _____

3. He also doesn't have any money because he's sometimes spent his income foolishly.
   _____
   _____

4. He bought a videocassette recorder last month because he isn't practical.
   _____
   _____

5. He didn't save any money, so he isn't able to buy some of the other things he wants now.
   _____
   _____

5 ▶ **Rewrite the sentences in brackets [ ] to give them more emphasis. Each sentence may be rewritten in two different ways.**

1. **A** What do you feel like doing tonight? Want to go to the concert at the Civic Center?
   B [I'd really like to see a movie.]

   What I'd really like to see is a movie.
   A movie is what I'd really like to see.

2. **A** *Dreams* is playing in both Westfield and Northfield. I think I'd rather go to Northfield. Is that O.K. with you?
   B I guess it would be all right, but [I'd rather go to Westfield.]

   _____

   _____

3. **A** Hmm, there's a movie on television that stars Gary Gabel. Are you interested?
   B Actually, [I'd like to see Cary Cable.] Is there anything playing that he's in?

   _____

   _____

4. **A** *Fright Night* is playing this week. Want to go?
   B That wouldn't be bad, but [I'd prefer to see *Night Fright*] if it's still around.

   _____

   _____

6 ▶ **Rewrite the movie review, changing each pair of sentences in brackets [ ] to a sentence with a nonrestrictive relative clause.**

***[**Deserted** is one of the best movies of the year. It opened at Cinema City last night.] [It's the second film directed by Tienne Dubois. She's the most exciting director now working.] [It stars Patricia Wen and Leonardo Amato. He's Ms. Dubois's husband in real life.] [**Deserted** is also a moving love story. It's advertised as a mystery.] [Patricia Wen plays a woman whose husband suddenly and mysteriously disappears. She gives the performance of her career.] [Alone, she begins her search for her husband. Her search takes her to North Africa.] [In Marrakesh, she is joined by her husband's brother. Her husband never told her about him.] The identity of this "brother" is only one of the mysteries in this must-see movie. Don't miss it!

Deserted, which opened at Cinema City last night, is one of the best movies of the year.

_____

_____

_____

_____

_____

_____

_____

7 ▶ **Attempt to persuade these people. Use the strategies in parentheses.**

1. You're the principal of a high school. You want Hannah Beker, one of the English teachers, to teach an extra class for the rest of the school year.

    a. (hard) *If you don't teach this class, Ms. Beker, I won't be able to recommend that you get a raise next year.*

    b. (soft) _____

    _____

    c. (rational) _____

    _____

2. You want your sister or brother to help you with your English homework.

    a. (hard) _____

    _____

    b. (soft) _____

    _____

    c. (rational) _____

    _____

8 ▶ **You're a teacher who needs more time to finish preparing for your 10:00 class. Make the following requests.**

1. Ask your principal whether you can have someone else take your 9:00 class.

    _____

    _____

2. Ask another teacher to take over your 9:00 class during his or her free period.

    _____

    _____

9 ▶ **A friend of yours has a sister who doesn't want to study English. Complete the sentences below with reasons why she should study it.**

1. It's important *for her to know English because she'll have more job possibilities.*

2. It's important that _____

    _____.

3. It's necessary _____

    _____.

4. It's essential that _____

    _____.